GREAT COA(

A compendium

self-coaching resource,

Nick Howell

GREAT COACHING QUESTIONS

TABLE OF CONTENTS

INTRODUCTION

WATCH ANY NEWS, political programme or interview and listen to the type and nature of the questions asked. What do you notice? What I see, is that generally, people are inherently poor when it comes to formulating questions that are effective, useful and powerful. I hear lots of closed questions; leading, emotive, long questions, statement and agenda-based questions too. Sadly, this is all too often replicated within our organisations as well. People are generally poor at asking good questions. Most people have never received development in how to ask effective, meaningful questions. If questioning skills are weak then this affects the passage of information and relationships and also performance of individuals, teams and organisations.

> *"To ask the right question is harder than to answer it."*
>
> GEORG CANTOR, MATHEMATICIAN.

Effective questioning and the formation of powerful questions is a learned activity. Learned in the moment and through deliberate reflection. The purpose of effective questions is to raise awareness, develop insight, provide information and promote understanding, in order to enable discovery and learning. Questioning is a fundamental skill for all coaches and leaders, it underpins how they operate and what they seek to achieve for their clients and employees. People new to practicing coaching often struggle to develop meaningful questions in the moment. Instead, they default to more closed questions or recycle similar questions on a regular basis with the same clients. Whilst some of these questions might hit the mark, being able to bring variety, depth, flexibility and quality to questioning is a critical coaching skill. Similarly, whilst experienced coaches will develop their own approaches and repertoire of questions, they too can fall into less productive, stale and unhealthy questioning habits.

The online Cambridge Dictionary defines a question as simply: *'a sentence or phrase used to find out information'*.

This is not a unique definition; it is however a one-dimensional and linear way of considering such a powerful tool. If we consider 'what is a question?' through a coaching and leadership lens we get a very different and valuable shift in perspective.

Questions become something quite radical and transformational. In this view, questions transform into:
- Vehicles enabling coaches to develop understanding for themselves and clients
- Keys to unlock client thinking and progress
- Ways of stimulating creativity
- Methods of raising self-awareness

- Approaches to challenging thinking, mindsets, assumptions and behaviours
- Demonstrations of interest from one person to another
- Ways of engaging others in powerful conversation

In viewing questions like this we also identify and demonstrate how important questions are, not just in coaching but in work generally. The adage, 'words are powerful, use them wisely' is well known and we can adapt and apply this phrase to our questions, coaching and leadership. Questions can be very powerful and need to be used very wisely to get the best results for clients and employees.

> ## "It is not the answer that enlightens, but the question."
>
> **EUGENE IONESCO, PLAYWRIGHT.**

As coaches, we need to recognise how important it is that we not only consider the types of questions we use with our clients, but also how and when we use them. Nonchalantly asking ad hoc questions has little or no value. Questions based on the coach's needs and not the client's, disempower the nature and purpose of questions and will achieve limited results and change for the client. All questions should consider the client or employee's context, the purpose of the conversation and what will be done with the responses.

However, good questions don't just happen. To adapt an Aristotle quote, *'anyone can ask questions, but to ask the right question in the right way at the right time and for the right reasons, that's the hard part.'* Those well versed in creating effective questions have achieved this through being conscious of the conversational situation they are in, understanding what they want to achieve, then formulating the appropriate questions. Powerful questions come from deliberate focus and action.

This compendium serves to promote and enable powerful questioning skills for coaches and leaders.

PURPOSE OF, AND HOW TO USE THE COMPENDIUM

"Ask the right questions, if you are going to find the right answers."

VANESSA REDGRAVE

THE COMPENDIUM consists of over 2000 coaching-based questions. It has been created to:

◆ Develop conversation, thinking and improve the application of questions to coaching conversations and leadership activities.

◆ Stimulate consideration of the 'right' questions asked in the right way, for the right situation and with the right intent, for the benefit of clients or employees.

◆ Help unblock thinking around questioning and the application of questions.

◆ Broaden coaches' and leaders' own awareness of the array and nature of powerful everyday questions that can be created.

◆ Challenge and inform questioning practices of coaches and leaders

◆ Be used as a way of self-coaching. Taking situations and applying questions to them to achieve more awareness and personal change.

If you're a line manager or leader who needs to develop your questioning skills, you'll find this compendium a valuable tool. Helping you develop confidence in question creation, deliver stronger approaches to organisational conversations and use questions as enabling tools for employees.

The questions in the compendium are primarily self-created. As a Coach, Coach Trainer and Coach Supervisor, I am always looking to understand what questions and lines of questioning work within client-coaching conversations. I work with new coaches to explore and examine their approach to questioning. I understand how impactful their questions can be and what value they add to the client and the conversation. This is all in order to develop good questioning practice. Within coaching qualification supervision conversations, I discuss how to utilise questions in different ways to achieve results with clients. How to reframe and rework questions into more tailored, beneficial and outcome-generating ones. How to translate closed limiting questions, into open and illu-minating ones.

The compendium serves to encourage reflective practice in leaders and coaches by reflecting on conversations and situations and the effectiveness of their questions and approaches. It draws out what learning can be taken from their questioning experience and adds it to the next experience. It considers how appropriate questions were, and how they can adapt or improve questioning techniques. It even reflects on how comfortable they were in asking the questions. The majority of questions and questioning techniques can be tweaked to the coach and client's style and preferences.

As coaches we find ways of using language and questions we are comfortable with. Some of the questions detailed you might not normally use, or form in the same way. Perhaps they don't work with your natural style. That's ok. You can adapt the questions to your own style and language. It is also worth remembering that whilst some questions might not fit with your style, that style might work with your clients. The coach needs to be flexible to meet their client's needs and preferences. Over time and reflection, you will learn to recognise what style of questions work best with your clients.

I have tried to reduce repetition of questions within the different areas to an absolute minimum. Sometimes I believe it is important to show the same question in different scenarios, as in the chapter 'Stakeholders' for example. It is equally valid to consider stakeholder-type questions within the 'Reality' section of GROW, or within 'Systemic questions.'

NOTES ON THE QUESTIONS

The questions are orientated towards work rather than life situations. They are organisationally based but not aimed towards specific organisational situations.

The questions are presented in a list format, simply for ease of access. The intent is for the coach to consider the client, context and their intent around the questions to choose the best environment for their use. Some books around questioning will describe where and how the questions could be used. This resource trusts in the coach's and leader's own judgment to make their own interpretation and application.

I have grouped questions into logical themes, types and exploration areas which I believe they work well in. There is also a natural flow to these groups, laid out as they might be used in a coaching conversation. I acknowledge you might argue the questions are not true 'X' questions. Or, they need to be under a different heading. This reflects our own experiences and interpretations. Similarly, you might believe that there should be categories included which I haven't. Based on my experience as a Coach and Coach Trainer I created categories which I found naturally or regularly occurred within coaching conversations, but these are not exclusive, nor complete.

Some of the questions might also seem very similar, however there are deliberately different nuances within some, which on the surface might seem the same.

There are no 'why' questions within the compendium. As a coach, I feel that these types of questions risk being misinterpreted and potentially cause conflict in the conversation. Similarly I have not considered closed questions in the compendium. There is absolute value in well-considered and deliberate closed questions. However open questions will form the majority of a coach's repertoire. This is where development will be greatest. There are no pure awareness-raising or problem-solving questions directly listed as a book chapter. In effect, all the questions, by their nature contribute to the awareness-raising and problem-solving process for the client.

Where I have taken questions from other sources, I have cited the source. In some of the questions, alternate options are provided e.g. reports/team/organisation. This is to demonstrate the different contexts which the question can be used or considered. Some of the questions might also be 'build' questions and align to the next ones in the list, where one question might naturally lead to subsequent ones when discussing a situation. These help further exploration and understanding with the client.

DISCLAIMERS

I do recognise that good questions are only half the answer. Good questions arise from deliberate focused and purposeful listening. The compendium allows coaches to absorb many questions and use it as a response to their diligent listening of the client, their situation and needs. Deep and purposeful listening enables the coach to understand the minutiae of client detail and consider this in their question creation. This kind of listening reduces the likelihood of building assumptions and biases into subsequent questions.

As a coach you might argue that questions used in coaching conversations should 'emerge' and be intuitive, based upon what the client brings to them. It might be said that having these questions risks removing spontaneity which doesn't allow for, as a friend described, the 'dancing in the moment', with the client. As a coach, I wholly concur with this sentiment and concern. The compendium is not meant to replace this spontaneity. Instead, anyone who uses this compendium and is conscious about developing their questioning technique and style is likely to assimilate many of the questioning approaches. They can then more unconsciously to bring quality questions to bear, allowing them to more confidently 'dance in the moment'.

A coach who simply brings a list of questions to the client is working from their own agenda, not the clients. The compendium is not meant to be used as a list, simply to reel questions from and fire at clients. Nor is it about using questions to be clever or eloquent in front of clients or employees. It is a core resource to support meaningful communication, increase understanding around questioning and further client growth.

I don't pretend to have a monopoly on what a complete set of questions is. The compendium is not meant to be complete or exhaustive. That is the joy of questions, they are ever-growing and evolving, tailored by the unique nature of every questioner, coach, leader, client and situation.

Will this compendium resource revolutionise coaching? No it will not. But, it will provide many new and experienced coaches with increased confidence to explore, expand and play with questions in their coaching practice. It will enable reflection and influence approaches and develop habits that help continually evolve as a coach. It will enable leaders to develop confidence in becoming questioning, inquisitive and people-centric leaders.

WHERE TO USE THE COMPENDIUM

THE FORMAT and approach is designed to present simple, practical one-line questions with complexity removed. Coaching questions should be simple and have clear purpose. The majority of questions are of an 'open' nature, with one or two statement questions, such as 'describe to me...' or 'tell me...'.

FOR COACHES THE COMPENDIUM WILL:

◆ Enable you to develop a wider repertoire of questions. Take the opportunity to read through, process and unconsciously absorb the questions. Perhaps, capture a few key questions in their coaching notes and preparation which you feel will be useful in your next session, or resonate with your client's context. Consciously consider different scenarios you have or might come across and where the questions or themes might be useful.

◆ Support you in planning your initial coaching sessions if you are a new coach. Being able to have a few opening and open questions can build confidence for you and the client. Having questions in your 'back pocket' for situations you might not be comfortable with will also be useful.

- Stimulate your thought processes when faced with particular situations or challenges to develop questioning approaches or strategies. Recognising that a client would gain value in having an area explored in more detail, or they avoid certain situations, or are not very expressive is a useful skill. The compendium can help plan and gain clarity in potential approaches to these. Creating thoughts around potential 'what if' and 'how could I' scenarios the client might bring and how you might explore through deliberate and different questioning options.
- Stimulate the creation of your own questions and lines of questioning.
- Help you reflect on your own approach to questions by recognising themes and habits if you are an experienced or developing coach. This provides opportunity to expand or evolve your questioning techniques, bringing scrutiny to your own professional practice.
- Encourage you to get feedback on your questioning skills, in order to then improve your questioning technique via the compendium.

If you coach infrequently, the compendium is a great way to refresh and remind yourself regarding this critical skill. Getting back into practice and at the same time reducing risk to the client and coaching conversation.

AS A LEADER THE COMPENDIUM WILL:

◆ Enable you to assess then hone your general questioning skills.
◆ Prepare you for workplace situations, generating questions that will add value to all involved.
◆ When considering a situation as a leader, simply reading through the questions can test the robustness of your thinking, approaches and actions undertaken. A form of self-coaching.

Broaden your repertoire of questions and their use in a wider range or organisational situations and people.

THE QUESTIONING LEADER

HISTORICALLY AND TRADITIONALLY, organisational leaders have focused on getting answers or on giving answers to those who surround them. Organisations have created leader centric working and thinking. Employees will go to their leaders and managers to seek direction, input, ideas and authority. Contemporary thinking around leadership recognises that the leader is but one person. Ideas, answers and performance lie within the team. Leaders lead teams of experts, and to do this well is not about providing answers but utilising this expertise.

"A question not asked, is a door not opened."

MARILEE GOLDBERG, THE ART OF THE QUESTION.

Many leaders do ask questions, but often these questions are transactional and tactical, about information, updates and reporting, or to solve a perceived problem. It is fair to say that the majority of leaders and managers have never received development in the effective use and power of deliberate questioning. Many forget that these skills are vital and should be honed to be more impactful and useful to those around them.

One of the common definitions of leadership is about *'achieving with and through other people' (Anon)*. For leaders to achieve with and through others they need to be comfortable in the realm of questions and questioning. Questions when asked with positive intent, enable and empower others. Highly effective leaders recognise that real power lies outside of themselves. That the only way to utilise this power is by asking questions (and listening of course). There can be no other way. They question and then they purposefully listen and repeat the cycle. Questioning takes focus away from leaders and expectations of them and brings others into the performance and solution arena.

Effective coaches and leaders are those who learn to 'park' their own egos and needs. By doing this it brings complete listening and questioning toward the employee, emphasising their importance. Putting them at the centre of the conversation and not the leader. This brings a complete shift in mindset, approach and language from the leader.

As with coaching, for a leader the ability to question effectively brings clarity, creativity, change, certainty, innovation and confidence. Both to themselves and others. It allows employees and leader to understand each other better, how they think and feel, reduce assumptions and minimise risk. Questioning raises the collective consciousness and ability. Questions unlock personal team and organisational value.

People generally like people who are interested in them. How many times have you had a work or social conversation (or been on a date...) and at the end of it you wished the person had shown more interest in you or asked more questions? Leaders who genuinely question, demonstrate curiosity and interest in others, this generates motivation and engagement. Using questions helps create trust and turns employees into followers of leaders.

Enabling others to be successful requires leaders to ask more challenging and probing questions. Stretching people in this way is rewarding for both parties, developing more personal accountability and ownership. Leaders need people in their team whose expertise is utilised and have the autonomy to deliver individual and team results. Questioning is a key to unlocking potential and translating it into performance.

Dani Buckley (2018) on the website *Center for Sales Strategy* shares key tips for leaders around questioning that aid both leader and employee:

- Ask one question at a time.
- Genuinely listen and care about the answer.
- Ask real questions that you actually want answers to.
- Ask follow up questions when it makes sense.
- Ask questions to help them share what they already know.
- Ask about things you don't know the answer to already.
- Return a question back to the asker if it is something they are equipped to answer on their own.

Additionally, I add:
- Ask questions people will enjoy answering!

By asking great questions, it brings out great answers and develops greatness in others. Leaders need to become great questioners for the benefit of others.

> *"Judge a man by his questions,*
> *not his answers."*

VOLTAIRE, WRITER.

Finally, by immersing themselves in the realm of questioning, leaders also develop and add value to themselves. By questioning and exploring, leaders are continually learning and becoming more self-aware. Good questions require deliberate thought which in turn enhances personal reflection. They also help develop a leader's emotional intelligence (EI) touching all of Daniel Goleman's (1995) EI elements of self-awareness, self-regulation, motivation, empathy and social skills.

Questions and questioning transforms leadership.

QUESTIONING FRAMEWORKS

QUESTIONING FRAMEWORKS and taxonomies are commonly used within education to help guide teacher's questioning (Hannel & Hannel 2004, Morgan and Saxton 2001 et al). These frameworks focus on active learning. One of the most commonly referenced is Bloom's Taxonomy (1956) (revised by Anderson and Krathwol in 2001). The 6-level hierarchy provides a comprehensive approach and set of measures to questioning to enable learning—*knowledge, comprehension, application, analysis, synthesis* and *evaluation*. Each level is dependent on the one prior.

This taxonomy is useful in reminding us as coaches, firstly, that there is no 'silver bullet' question. Secondly, that questions often need to be progressive to bring out most learning. Indeed, there is synergy between the language of the taxonomy levels and that which is often used in coaching models. Both are progressive in nature.

It is very easy to just think up random questions, but, just because you think of a question doesn't mean it will be of value to the client. Questions that are considered, relevant, tailored and stretching are the most powerful. Whilst coaches utilise coaching models to help frame their questions and exploration with clients, there is key value knowing and embracing Bloom's Taxonomy.

Utilising it in question formation to deliberately help develop client thinking and progress their learning.

Questions within the compendium can be identified to align with the taxonomy's levels. Similarly, the compendium questions can be adapted accordingly to enable progression through it. Key words have been identified for each of the levels. These key words can be used to help formulate (measurable) questions for clients.

LEVEL	KEY WORDS
Knowledge	what, who, when, name, list, tell, state, show, identify
Comprehension	describe, explain, summarise, compare, clarify, express, estimate
Application	Demonstrate, construct, show, relate, consider, choose
Analysis	Compare, contrast, separate, illustrate, predict, show, analyse
Synthesis	Create, design, devise, develop, explain, compose, propose, plan
Evaluation	Justify, compare, conclude, evaluate, estimate, assess, choose, describe

TYPES OF QUESTIONS

BEFORE EXAMINING individual questions under their different themes, it is worth recognising that there are many different types of questions. Each type of question has a different purpose, focusing client thinking in different ways, bringing out specific answers. From these types, coaches can naturally form their individual questions pertinent to their clients. Whilst we may not overtly remember the question types, awareness of them is important. An array of these is listed below, recognising that there may be many more and varying interpretations of them.

- *Probing*
- *Clarification*
- *Rhetorical*
- *Testing*
- *Convergent*
- *Divergent*

- *Comparison*
- *Application*
- *Analysis*
- *Leading*
- *Interpretive*
- *Factual*

- *Conceptual*
- *Awareness raising*
- *Evaluative*
- *Hypothetical*

In the compendium we will touch on all these types of questions. With awareness of your client it is for you to determine which to use, where to use them and how to develop your questions from them.

USING THIS COMPENDIUM AS A SELF-COACHING RESOURCE

WHILST COACHING is primarily about one person coaching another, self-coaching is a perfectly viable and valuable activity. In its simplest form, it works on the basis of using your own skills to examine your own situation and needs. Building your self-awareness and self-reflection to change an aspect of your work or life. It requires you to be both coach and client at the same time—a big juggling act!

As such it requires focus, deliberate attention as well as discipline to achieve high quality results. Allocating time, planning and intent to it just as you would in a one-on-one coaching scenario. Being able to add value by using your 'inner coach' at any time to examine something and get clarity or direction. The difficulty around self-coaching is how to identify, ask and respond to our own challenging questions. Then seeing the elements and themes that an external perspective would more readily identify.

Coaching is about identifying what needs to be achieved, developed or changed, whilst understanding and exploring the situation, then putting new actions in place to bring the desired change. Helping to move a person from where they are to where they want or need to be. In self-coaching you are only accountable to yourself so at times it can be hard to put next steps in place and ensure they are completed. Self-coaching requires discipline, sticking to a chosen process or framework and practicing.

A key to self-coaching is to capture the outputs of the questions. Notes, mind maps or post-it notes captured at the time allow for subsequent processing, reflection, understanding then action.

> *"My philosophy is that not only are you responsible for your life but doing the best at this moment puts you in the best place for the next moment."*
>
> OPRAH WINFREY, TV HOST.

Developing familiarity and practice with coaching techniques and tools will enable more effective self-examination, exploration and self-challenge. Enabling greater objectivity in situations and forcing you to approach and think about things differently to how you would normally.

Some top tips to make self-coaching work for you:

◆ Capture all of your thinking—notes, mind maps or post-it notes will allow you to subsequently process, reflect and understand.

◆ Ask the right question—it's not about asking lots of questions to yourself, but asking the right questions, the ones which might challenge or open up your thinking. If you see a question and it resonates with you—use it!

◆ Be patient—sometimes the best answers come, not in the moment but when our brain is relaxed. Take your time both in using the questions and in answering them.

◆ Small steps—don't try and 'boil the ocean'. Work and commit to manageable pieces.

◆ It's ok not get it right first time. Be kind to yourself. Learning comes from both getting it right and wrong.

◆ Take some ownership—the situation is yours to own work through and resolve. The responsibility is yours. Take control.

◆ Get support—having someone simply share what you are doing or even be accountable to will feel like the load is being lightened.

◆ Step out—try doing your self-coaching in places outside of your normal environment. Being in different places is stimulating. Go for a walk and in different parts focus on different questions and situations, capture your thoughts in a small notebook.

- Get insight from others—seeking feedback from those who know you, or people affected by your changes. They will help to see things you might miss by yourself.
- Celebrate success!—when changes occur, however small, it is right and proper to recognise what you have achieved. Take time to look up and smile at your success.

With regular practice, self-coaching can become a habitual and unconscious activity applicable to a range of work and life scenarios. Additionally, making a habit of asking yourself questions will also naturally enhance your outward questioning skills, toward external situations and people.

The compendium can be a vehicle for self-coaching, exploring, asking questions, developing understanding and taking action yourself. Leader or employee, it is equally applicable.

Here are three suggested approaches to developing a self-coaching practice through the compendium:

1. COMPENDIUM PRIME QUESTIONS

To make self-coaching a little more accessible most chapters have a set of suggested prime self-coaching questions that you can use individually or in their entirety. These will help you bring focus to your self-coaching. Regular use of these will build confidence in your ability to self-coach and also stepping out and formulating your own self-coaching questions.

It can be tempting when self-coaching to only ask and answer the 'easy' questions. These prime questions remove this risk, bringing deliberate and stretching thinking.

2. UTILISING TGROW

Methodically approach your situation by reviewing and using the recognised TGROW model and questions in the later chapter as a step-by-step process. This will allow you to examine in detail your situation and then identify a variety of ways forward. Not all the questions in TGROW have to be used, pick ones most pertinent to you or your situation.

3. EVOLVING APPROACH

This approach is more fluid than the first two. It uses elements from many of the differing types of questions within the compendium. You will have to adapt the questions chosen from the chapters, switching the language from 'you' to 'I'. Here is a suggested process you could follow:

◆   Develop familiarity with the question chapters, knowing what each type of question is used for.

- Sit down and consider what it is you want to get from your own coaching. What is it you are trying to change or improve? Look at some of the **Framing** questions to stimulate this. These questions will bring some focus to the area you wish to explore. Combining the use of a few of these questions will incrementally refine the focus to develop a targeted coaching area.

- Get specific and know what it is you want to achieve by using **Measure** questions. Do not progress from here until you have something tangible in the way of measuring the success of your own self-coaching. What do you need/want to come away from the coaching with? What will be the tangible change or shift you are looking for? Measures will help to demonstrate progress and provide motivation.

- Next, move on to using some of the **Person-Centred** questions. These will allow exploration and tailoring of thinking about the situation in the context of you, your needs and wants. These questions will be very challenging, bringing internal scrutiny.

- If there is some personal angst or emotions around the situation **Feeling and Thinking** questions can help to understand these emotions more clearly. Feelings and thoughts underpin behaviours and performance and so are important to understand and consider.

- **Creative** questions will allow for new or different ways forward to be identified. Often, we will simply approach situations as we always have, in the same language and style, which can be unproductive. Creative questions force you to think differently and imaginatively.
- If there is real feeling of being stuck, **Unblocking** or **Magical** questions can be very effective.
- **Commitment** questions can be used to identify actions that focus on achieving outcomes.
- Once you have come to the end of this process you need to identify when you are going to begin applying some of these new ways and check in with your initial **Measure** questions, to see if you have achieved the success you set out to.
- After your self-coaching and application of your new ways, **Reflective** questions will bring further learning out of your experiences. Especially when combined with seeking feedback from others who are in a position to observe your changes and bring further awareness and learning.

SOCRATIC QUESTIONING

AS THE NAME hints at, this questioning approach has its origins with the Greek philosopher and educator, Socrates. He reputedly taught by asking questions of his pupils in order to draw out answers from them. The intent and purpose of his questioning was to bring focus, challenge and accuracy to his pupil's thinking. In doing so this allowed his students to consider ideas logically and check their validity in order to get closer to the 'truth'. Socratic questioning is still promoted as a way for teachers to work with their pupils.

This way of critical questioning brings depth to discussions and independent thinking for your coaching client. Taking their short or automatic responses and using logic going beneath the surface of them, deliberately examining for meaning, thinking and logic to bring out the fullest possible understanding.

Socratic questions are ideal for you as coach or leader as they work from the basis of you demonstrating 'ignorance' on the topic. This reduces the risk of leading or bringing in your own opinions and biases to the conversation.

Whilst the questions are powerful, they shouldn't be solely relied upon in the coaching process. Instead, consider using them when you are wishing to explore particular situations or comments more deeply and progressively.

There are deliberate Socratic questions below, however there are individual ones scattered throughout the compendium too.

COACHING TIPS:
- The use of silence with some of these questions can be very powerful, encouraging and allowing the client to be present in their own thoughts. Drawing out further thinking that might otherwise be lost by moving on too quickly.
- By following up with a further **Socratic** or **Person-Centred** question linked to the client's response will reveal further layers and 'flavour' to the discussion.

Clarification—getting your clients to think more about their position and being clearer about what it is they are looking at or considering. Bringing more deliberate accuracy to the conversation and their points:

◆ The reasons you are saying that are what?
◆ What do you mean when you say X?
◆ What is your main point?
◆ What does this mean?
◆ How does this relate to what you have been sharing?
◆ What do you already know here?
◆ What do you already know about this person/situation?
◆ Explain that point further would you?
◆ What examples do you have?
◆ How might you rephrase that?
◆ What do you mean by...?
◆ How do you feel about this?
◆ What are you talking about here, this..., or this...?

Challenging assumptions—often assumptions will be made by clients, either caused by the situation or because they are more deeply held by the client as unquestioned beliefs. This may cloud thinking, reduce focus and limit direction and solutions. Making simple pointed challenges forces the client to revisit and examine their current thinking and words:

◆ What are the other points of view here?
◆ How did you come to this assumption?

- How much is this always the situation?
- Explain to me your thoughts here?
- Where does that assumption originate from?
- What are you assuming?
- What assumptions might you be making here?
- What do you need to assume?
- What exceptions might there be?
- What might happen if...?
- What needs to be challenged here?
- What do you need to challenge in your own thinking?
- What would challenging that thinking bring you?
- What would others challenge you on here?
- What challenge might others bring to what you are saying here?

Evidence and reasoning—helping your client to strengthen their position by ensuring that they have evidence or a reasoned basis to support their position. Ensuring it comes from a strong factual basis:

- What examples have you go to support this?
- How do you know?
- How can you prove that?
- What do you have that validates what you say?
- What do you know that validates this?
- What is causing this to happen?
- What is your logic behind that question/comment/thinking?
- What makes you think this is true?

- What doubt can you bring to this?
- How robust is that evidence for you?
- What leads you to think this?
- How much would this stand up to scrutiny?
- How might you counter this argument?
- What evidence is there to counter this?
- How sure are you of what you are saying?
- What do you need convincing of here?
- How might others challenge this?
- How sufficient is this to base a decision?
- What makes this happen?
- What authority do you have to say that?

Alternate viewpoints—the intent here is to broaden your client's perspective and consider varying ways of viewing a situation or issue. It's not uncommon for clients to have conditioned, blinkered and distinct views over situations. Here, you get the client to appreciate a myriad of other perspectives:

- What are some alternative viewpoints to this?
- What are the other viewpoints on this?
- What is the counter viewpoint here?
- What are the different perspectives on this?
- How do you need to see this differently?
- How many other views are there on this?
- How could you view this differently?
- If I forced you to see this from another perspective, what would that be?
- What is the flip side of looking at this?
- Who is likely to benefit from this?

- How could others view this?
- How different is this to...?
- How is this better than...?
- How does this compare to...?
- How necessary is...?

Implications and consequences—clients can get very engrossed in a situation or focused on particular ideas and direction. Almost a 'target fixation'. Through these questions you encourage the client to consider the impact of their thinking or approaches in order to generate alternatives or test the robustness of their argument:

- What would be the consequences here?
- What might be the consequences here?
- What might happen if you pursue this route?
- What will happen here?
- How might this affect others?
- What are the short term implications of this?
- What are the longer term effects?
- What is important here?
- What does this mean for you/others?
- What are the knock-on effects here?
- What now happens because of this?
- How far is the reach of this?
- What might happen if you didn't do/say this?
- What might be the risks of that decision?
- What are the ripple effects of this?
- What is best here?
- How does X affect Y here?
- What is best for you/others here?

Challenging the question—the purpose here is to generate indirect critical analysis and thinking with your client. Getting them to read between the lines, interpret and extrapolate from the immediate question or conversation:

- What was important about that question?
- The reasons this question is important are what?
- Where do you think my question came from then?
- What might have been a different question to ask?
- What was the point of me asking you that?
- What might you draw from that question?
- What else might I ask here?
- Where else does this question take you?
- What else does this question surface for you?
- What other questions could be asked around this?
- What question did you want me to ask instead of that one?
- What is your thinking behind this?

CONTRACTING THE RELATIONSHIP

All coaches know the importance of contracting with new clients and agreeing how they are going to work together for the duration of the coaching assignment. Developing this psychological contract also begins to establish mutual awareness, understanding and trust.

Many new and existing coaches treat contracting simply as a process or exercise to go through. It then becomes a monologue like transaction, rather than a discussion and mutual discovery. Contracting is also an investment in nurturing the client relationship. Sharing information in contracting, getting to know each other combined with considered questions transform the nature of the conversation and its outputs.

Contracting is an information gathering activity, helping inform your coaching, style and language toward the client. You also begin to create a picture of how engaged the client is likely to be in the assignment. Clients for themselves also gather vital information about you, the coaching process and their role in the relationship. Contracting well via questions engages the client and they become more involved in it. Your contracting reduces risk for all parties.

Though not covered in the compendium, it is recognised that consideration should be given to 3-way and even wider stakeholder contracting.

I strongly believe that contracting is made up of two strands. The elements that are absolutes to cover—confidentiality, logistics, roles etc. Then there are elements and areas that are useful to consider, which add value to the coaching—discussing values and beliefs, approaches to learning, their motivation etc. These form a further psychological contract with the client; how the coach is going to approach and work with the client.

Core questions support contracting conversations—there is lot of core information that the client needs to understand to help them embrace the coaching. Involving your client by using questions to tease out some of this information introduces them to the coaching approach as creating a stronger agreement between parties:

- What's your understanding of coaching and how it works?
- What's important about confidentiality for us in our coaching?
- What confidentiality needs to be in place?
- What do you think falls outside of confidentiality between us?
- What is the purpose of the coaching for you?
- What is it you ultimately wish to achieve by undertaking the coaching?

- What is your overall goal for the coaching?
- What might be the components of this overall goal?
- What involvement do you want to have in organising the sessions?
- Who else needs to be aware of the coaching?
- What will you share with them about it?
- What do they need to know about it?
- What does your line manager need to know about it?
- What discussions have been had with your line manager about the coaching?
- What do you need to tell them about it?
- How do you want to have your manager involved?
- What are your reasons for not sharing about the coaching with them?
- What value might they be able to bring to your development?
- Outside of me what support do you have?
- What support do you think you might need?
- Where can you seek feedback from to give your insight on your progress during the coaching?
- What is it you are ultimately trying to achieve from the coaching?
- Who is best placed to provide you with feedback on your progress?
- What is your commitment to the coaching?
- How committed are you to your coaching?
- How will your commitment show itself during our time together?
- What commitment do you think you need to bring to the coaching?

- What support would you like from me between sessions?
- What kind of communication happens between us between sessions?
- What might stop you from putting actions in place from our coaching?
- How can you reduce the likelihood of this happening?
- What do you need from me during the coaching?
- What else do I need to know from you before we agree to start the coaching?
- What else might be useful to share with me before we begin?
- What questions do you have around the coaching, process or me as your coach?
- At the end, how will you know if the coaching has been successful/worked?
- What will be different for you at the end of the coaching?

Value adding contracting questions—the contracting meeting presents an opportunity to start to establish and develop the client relationship. It also is a time to learn how your client thinks, learns and communicates, in order to mirror and utilise this in conversations:

- How do you like to approach learning new things?
- What would be good to know about you that might help the coaching?
- What else would be good to know about you before we engage in the coaching?
- What's important to you about this coaching?

- How do I develop a coaching relationship with you?
- What are some of your values and beliefs that might surface or be challenged during the coaching?
- What approaches or styles have you noted about others that do not work for you?
- How are you about sharing your thoughts and feelings about something?
- How would you respond if I asked you questions about your thoughts and feelings?
- What are you like at receiving challenge?
- How receptive are you to feedback?
- What are you like at receiving feedback from someone?
- How would you like us to work together during the coaching?
- If you have undertaken personality profiles, what have they revealed about you?
- If you have undertaken personality profiles, what have you learnt from them?
- How do the profiles/preferences describe you?
- What colours come out in the assessments you have undertaken?
- What 360 feedback have you ever received that might be useful to be aware of?

RE-CONTRACTING

THERE IS A PHRASE in coaching that goes 'contract early and often'. Yes, we contract at the start of the intervention. But we also re-contract anytime there is a change in the relationship or coaching, either from them or us. This ensures that we maintain the relationship's integrity and reduce risk to both parties:

- What has changed since our last conversation that we need to recontract on?
- What has changed in the relationship that we might need to recontract?
- What now do you think needs to be re-contracted?
- How does this now affect or change our coaching dialogue?
- How does this now change how we work together?
- What did we agree on in the contracting regarding commitment to the coaching?
- What has shifted here from what we originally contracted on?
- How might we look to recognise these changes in our coaching relationship?
- What are the reasons we might now need to re-contract?
- Because of what you just shared what might we now need to do in our coaching?
- In light of this change, what needs to happen in our conversation?

- What are your thoughts on re-visiting our original contracting discussion?
- How do we look to re-contract this?
- As your role/reporting has now changed, who might we need to bring into a contracting conversation?
- How does what you have shared here impact on our contracted relationship?
- Before discussing this, what might we need to consider around the contracting conversation we had?

FRAMING YOUR FOCUS

INITIAL FRAMING QUESTIONS are designed to help your client determine and shape the area they want or need to talk about. Often, clients can come to the conversation with a broad, generic or even a mixed picture of what they believe they want to discuss. The client may also 'present' a discussion area, something they believe you will want them to talk about, rather than what they actually need to talk about. It can be confusing exactly what the 'field of play' is. If not correctly understood, later in the conversation it may transpire that this wasn't really the area they needed to talk about, and the process has to restart. If your and their focus is too broad, the rest of the conversation may lack clarity and direction. It will also impact upon the creation of the actual coaching goal and making identification of appropriate options and actions difficult.

It is important for you to work hard initially to tease out the primary focus area for the conversation.

Sometimes, the client doesn't know how to express their situation, focus area and wants. It therefore lies with the coach to explore from different angles to help them fully express their focus area to help them create their own picture and truer understanding. These capitalise questions enable you to explore the topic areas from differing angles gaining clarity for both parties.

ALSO CONSIDER:

Framing questions are not too dissimilar to Topic questions listed in the **TGROW** chapter. However, Topic questions may tend to be broader in nature, whereas Framing ones begin to distil down the focus more. Coaches can go from Framing to Goal in the GROW model.

Discussion Framing—simple open questions which invite the client to bring to the table whatever they wish. There may be some direction encouraged in the question. Or, you include a focussed word which may help stimulate their thinking on areas for discussion. The coach might choose to use a version of some of these questions initially in their contracting conversation, to get a broader sense of the coaching focus:

- What do you want to discuss and the reasons for this?
- What's on your mind today?
- What's on your mind today that you would like to discuss?
- What specifically do you want to talk about here today?
- How do you want to use our time together today?
- What are you bringing to the table to discuss today?
- What would be most useful to bring to the table in the session?
- What would be most useful to discuss today?

- If you wanted to talk about something today what would it be?
- What are you bringing to the table to discuss today?
- Where do we need to spend our 90 minutes today?
- What's important for you to talk about today?
- What do you need to talk about today?
- What should be discussed here?
- What should we be talking about today?
- What's the easier area to talk about today?
- What's the more challenging or uncomfortable area to talk about?
- Which of your work areas would value being explored?
- What is the most value adding area to explore?
- What are the top 3/5 things you could discuss today?
- In our contracting conversation we broke your bigger goal into smaller chunks. Which chunk do you want to look at first?

Focus Framing—here, you attempt to bring clarity and distil areas down that can or should be discussed:

- What are the no-go areas for today's conversation?
- What is on topic and off topic in today's conversation?
- Out of all the things you have spoken about, what do you want to bring to the table?
- What is the order we might want to talk about things?
- What is the natural starting point for our conversation?

- Of all the things you have shared, which one(s) do we need to look at today?
- What are the natural priorities in what we look at first?
- What is the order of things to be discussed?

Challenge Framing—these questions raise the bar with your client, forcing them to give deliberate attention to where the coaching conversation needs to be. You are really challenging and pushing the client, testing their thinking:

- What are the likely achievements from the conversation?
- What do we need to focus on today to keep the momentum towards your goal?
- What is the difference between what you want to discuss versus what you need to discuss?
- What's most important that we look at today for you/your team/stakeholders?
- What would your stakeholders say is important to discuss today?
- What would your stakeholders suggest we don't talk about?
- How much is this area you want to look at a symptom or a cause?
- Which of these will have most impact on what you are trying to achieve?
- What do you need to talk about today as opposed to what you want to talk about?
- What must we talk about today?

- What are the main challenges you are facing at present?
- What could we focus on that will make the most difference to your situation?
- What is going to be valuable to discuss today from your team/a team perspective?
- What might your line manager want/need us to discuss together?
- What is causing you the most anxiety/pain which therefore should be a focus for us?
- What is most important that we attend to today?
- What does the team need the focus of the conversation to be?

TOP 10 FRAMING SELF-COACHING QUESTIONS

1. What specifically do I want to explore?
2. What do I need to resolve here?
3. What should I examine today that will have the most impact on the situation?
4. What are the key challenges I am facing?
5. What do I want to get out of this coaching time?
6. How do I maximise this time I have for myself?
7. Of the things I could focus on, which will add most value to me?
8. What should I focus on which will help me feel better about the situation?
9. What is the order I should focus on things?
10. What might be a distraction to what I should be considering?

TGROW COACHING MODEL

THERE IS AN ARRAY of coaching models used by coaches. The GROW model was popularised by John Whitmore in the early 1990's. GROW (Goal, Reality, Options and Wrap up) is the most commonly used coaching model with new coaches. It is a clear, structured and progressive process. It is well suited to the creation of effective questions within it. Myles Downey (2003) subsequently added the 'T' for Topic later to make TGROW.

Being able to bring a coaching model to life through well-considered questions is a critical coaching skill. In doing so it becomes a more engaging learning experience for clients. You simply formulate questions for each stage, not progressing forward in the model until your questions have brought sufficient awareness and outputs for client and coach. On the whole the TGROW process is linear, moving from Topic through to Wrap up; though there can be revisiting of some of the elements. For example, getting a little understanding of the Reality to help inform the Goal.

When using a coaching model, as a reflective coach you may begin to notice certain themes to your questions. Do you use the same cycle of questions at the same point of the model? Do you have default questions you go to? Do certain clients evoke certain questions from you? This set of TGROW questions are an opportunity to review, revise and add to your repertoire of model-based questions.

These questions also present an opportunity for you to stretch yourself by playing with and testing new questions, ones which you might not ordinarily use. This will develop confidence in a broader range of conversations with a model you are already familiar with.

COACHING TIP
Whilst the questions have been developed for TGROW, many are equally transferable to the other coaching models coaches might evolve to in the future.

Topic questions—working with your client to understand the focus area of conversation for the session. This is very much higher-level context setting, in order for the coach to have an initial understanding to then help tailor the goal. The use of **Framing** questions can also be considered here too:

- Tell me, what would you like to discuss today?
- What would you like to explore in today's session?
- From our last conversation, what would you like to focus on in our time together?
- How would you like to use our next 90 minutes?
- What could we discuss that would have most impact on you?

- What are your reasons for wanting to explore this topic?
- What issues do you want to work on today?
- How can I support you today?
- Thinking back to your original goal, what is the next element you would like to discuss?
- What brings you here today?
- What are you wanting to bring to your coaching today?
- How can I help you?
- What shall we talk about today?

Goal questions—the purpose here is for the you to tease out from the client what specifically they want to achieve from the conversation. What will be their take-aways, outcomes or outputs from the session? You need to spend time here to ensure both parties have absolute and equal clarity and understanding of the goal. This ensures they have the same focus and direction. It may take a while to shape the goal with the client:

- By the end of our time together, what do you want to have achieved?
- What is the purpose of today's meeting and topic you have shared?
- When we finish today, what outcomes do you want to go away with?
- What matters the most to you about this?
- Tell me what good would look like to you for you today?
- What outcome would make this conversation a great success? (Stoltzfus 2008)

- What outcome do you want to achieve today?
- What would you like to take away from this session?
- Describe your perfect outcome from this session.
- What would you like to see happen from today's session?
- What would be a valuable outcome for you today?
- In 3 months-time what do you want to have achieved?
- In 6 months, what would that look like?
- How do we turn what you want to achieve into a more measurable goal?
- What do you expect from me today?
- What results do you wish to accomplish today?
- Tell me about what a perfect result would be here?
- What would be a great outcome for you today?
- How will this conversation make a difference to you or your situation?
- How will this conversation take you closer to your goal today?
- What do you want to achieve here, today?
- What is important to you right now?
- What is most important to you right now?
- How will you measure your goal?
- What outcome would be ideal for you?
- Given your topic, what is it that needs to be different/change/ or improve?
- What do you REALLY want?
- What do you want to change?
- What would make today's session a success for you?
- How appropriate is this goal?
- How challenging is this goal for you?

- What result are you trying to achieve?
- How will you know if our time today has been well spent, what will be different?
- Describe your perfect world in relation to your situation.
- What is your goal for today's coaching session?

Reality questions—having established the purpose of the coaching conversation, the coach now has to gather information from the client about their present situation. Developing deeper understanding of what has been happening in and around the client in relation to their goal to date. Quality time here provides the coach with masses of useful information and allows them to explore, challenge, observe and provide feedback to the client:

- What is the current situation in relation to your goal?
- What meaning does this goal have for you?
- What will things look like when you are successful?
- Where are you at in relation to your goal currently?
- What do you want here?
- What are you not doing in relation to achieving your goal?
- What is happening at the moment for you?
- What influence is this having upon you?
- What has brought you to this point?
- Describe the situation/challenge a little more to me.
- What information are you looking for here?

- What's currently standing in your way from moving this forward?
- What will not happen if you don't do something here?
- What information is missing at the moment?
- What information do you need to make a decision or to move things forward?
- When did this last happen?
- What insights do you need to tease out?
- What existing skills, knowledge and experience can you draw upon to help you?
- What is important to you about this/this situation?
- What does 'X' look like to you?
- What does good/ideal/perfect look like here or to you?
- What is required of you?
- What has led you to being in this situation?
- What skills/knowledge might you need to develop?
- What skills/behaviours/knowledge are missing currently?
- What skills/behaviours/knowledge can you already bring to the situation?
- How might your thoughts/feelings be affecting you/the situation?
- What have you tried so far, how's it been going?
- Help me understand why this situation/change is important to you.
- What is happening NOW?
- How do you compare to others at this point?
- What has helped your progress to date?

- Tell me about what's been going on for you around this situation?
- What progress have you made so far?
- What steps have you taken so far?
- How are you thinking/feeling about the situation?
- What is working well right now for you?
- What information do you NOT have?
- What information have you gathered that might help you?
- What do you not know about (the situation)?
- How is it affecting the people around you/your team?
- How will you know if you have been successful here?
- What feedback from others will help you know if you have been successful?
- What do you need to change about the environment/situation?
- Where do you stand now?
- What is within your power here?
- What are the reasons you haven't achieved your goal already?
- What is causing this situation?
- Who must/needs to be involved in this?
- Who needs to be involved in the solution?
- What would be the benefits if you achieved this goal?
- What has contributed to your success(es) so far?
- How can you get what you need to start?
- What do you think is stopping you?
- How are things progressing for you?
- What do you think was really happening?

- What have you learnt so far?
- When/where did it start?
- On a scale of 1-10, how do you feel about the situation, with 10 being brilliant?
- On the scale, how do you want to feel?
- Describe how you feel about being an X? What is working/not working for you in this place?
- What are the challenges you are facing?
- If you achieve X, what would be different?
- What is required of you?
- How will you be thinking?
- What feedback would you be receiving?
- What is most important to you in this situation or in this relationship?
- What are the views of other stakeholders?
- What has been the feedback from stakeholders?
- What are the needs of the stakeholders?
- How are the stakeholders involved in this situation/with you?
- What do the stakeholders NOT want?
- How have you been communicating with your stakeholders?
- What influence do you have here?
- How have you been approaching the situation/issue up until now?
- How critical/urgent is the situation?
- What has worked/not worked for you?
- Who have you approached about this?
- Who else has been involved?
- What other factors might be involved here?
- What's most challenging for you about the situation?

- What did you learn from them?
- How could you turn this situation around?
- Share what you have considered perhaps due to cost, time, resources etc.
- What has been suggested to you?
- How is the situation affecting you?
- What will you need to do to change the situation?
- How else could we view this situation?
- How might others view it?
- What are others doing differently in other areas of the business?
- Share your thoughts on what has been tried so far.
- What would 'good' look like for you in this situation?
- What else would it be good for me to know about?
- Before we move on to options, what else needs to be shared?

Options questions—once a picture of the current situation for the client has been developed with the client, the coach then needs to help the client find new different or alternative ways forward. The skill for you is to develop creativity and lateral thinking through their questions. Stimulating the client to open their mind to wider ideas and approaches outside of their normal thinking patterns:

- What could you try?
- Where could you look for ideas?
- How could you change the situation?
- What might work here?
- What is in your gift/power to change?

- What are the possibilities here?
- What are the possibilities?
- Tell me about the possibilities around this.
- Tell me what you think/feel might happen if you tried doing that.
- What do you feel you should do differently?
- Who could share expertise or experience?
- If you could try anything here, what might it be?
- What is being tried in other areas of the business?
- If you had a wish list of possibilities, what would be on it?
- What might a colleague or friend suggest to you?
- Which opportunity(ies) are you going to pursue?
- What have you tried previously elsewhere, which might be useful here?
- Who might have ideas to support you in this?
- How will you turn your steps into a plan to follow?
- What would happen if you did nothing?
- How have you tackled this/situation before?
- What would you gain/lose by this/these options?
- What might an expert in this area consider?
- How might Google/a bank/supermarket approach this issue?
- What do you think you need to do next?
- What logically needs to happen?
- What if you had no limit on resources, how would that affect your thinking or actions?
- If you did nothing short/medium-term what will happen?
- Out of all these options, what is your gut feeling about the best one(s)?

- You have identified several possibilities, which stands out best and for what reasons?
- What guidance would you give to someone else about this situation?
- Who do you know who has come across a similar situation before?
- What is another option besides the ones you have brought out?
- If you knew the answer to this, what would it be?
- If you were to start this piece/project from scratch, how would you go about it?
- Ranking these options as the most effective/ quickest/most value adding/which would be in your top 3?
- Which ones need to come first?
- Tell me how you plan to overcome any obstacles
- Which might be best fit for you/your team?
- Which options appeal to you the most and why?
- What can be your next step?
- If you were to decide now, which is the best option here?
- If you chose this approach, what sort of things would you see happening in 6 months-time?
- Should you implement this choice, what would you see happening if it was the best choice?
- Which option(s) do you feel ready to act on?
- If you went for this option, what might be the implications for you?
- What else?
- Which of these options due you want to pursue?
- What are the consequences (positive and negative) of your chosen options?

- How would this approach affect the team?
- Taking X option, let's explore this. How would you apply it to see if it would work?

Wrap-up questions—bringing the conversation to a natural conclusion. This involves summarising the conversation, ensuring actions are identified, support determined, deadlines agreed, direction understood, and client commitment achieved. You are asking questions to ensure that when the client leaves the conversation, they have the clarity and motivation they need to achieve their actions:

- Tell me about your plans to bring your options to fruition.
- What might you need to consider before doing anything else?
- What do you plan to implement first?
- What does your manager/team need you to tackle first?
- Where is the best place to start?
- Where do you need to start with these options?
- What are your first actions or steps here?
- What are you willing to do to achieve this?
- What can you do to achieve this?
- How will you know if you have been successful with this option?
- What is your deadline for this action?
- How will you know you have done it?
- What needs to happen to move this forward?
- What is the order in which things need to happen?
- Where are you going to start?

- What will your measures of success be?
- How will others be measuring your success?
- What about any obstacles to you achieving these actions?
- Describe resistance you might experience.
- How will these options and actions help you achieve your goal?
- How will you ensure that you do these things?
- What needs to happen to get you there?
- Where might resistance come from?
- What are the natural steps to achieve and implement your options?
- What is the natural flow to your steps?
- Who can support you in this?
- Who has expertise to support you in this?
- What resources do you need?
- Outside of the coaching who is best placed to support you?
- What support do you need from me?
- What will happen if you don't do this?
- What will be the cost of not doing this?
- What will be affected if you don't achieve/do this?
- On a scale of 1-10, what is the likelihood of your plan succeeding?
- Looking at it now, how achievable are your plans and steps?
- On a scale of 1-10, how confident are you with achieving your actions?
- On a scale of 1-10 how motivated/committed are you to doing this?
- What would make it a 10?

IDENTIFYING MEASURES FOR COACHING

COACHING LIKE other business activities needs to have measures in place. Measures for the client, sponsor and organisation, and for you as the coach. Establishing measures at the start of the assignment gives you both a focal point, helping identify when success is achieved. They also help demonstrate the value added during the coaching intervention. You will need to help the client establish either quantitative or qualitative measures, as appropriate, or both. This may also be done with other stakeholders or the sponsor.

Exploration of initial measures, outcomes or successes are likely to begin in the contracting session, then continually revisited and reviewed throughout the coaching. Seeking feedback from the client and stakeholders ensures the coaching and outcomes are on track. Each set of measures will depend on the nature of the work, the role of the client, the purpose of the coaching and personal needs of the client.

Being able to get the client to effectively articulate these in a way they are both understandable and provide validity, requires accurate questioning by the coach.

Sometimes clients will not be able to fully articulate valid measures. Time diligently spent here will ensure measures are recognisable, relevant and achievable. Investing in quality measuring questions here directly influences the coach's subsequent approaches and the likelihood of success at the end.

The concept of measuring in the compendium is split into two areas—pre-coaching and changes. Both are different facets of measuring and each bringing value to the conversation and client.

Pre-coaching—Done prior to the formal coaching sessions, ideally during contracting. These measures can be used for both the achievement of the larger coaching goal and individual sessions too:

◆ How will you measure the success of the coaching?
◆ What will be different for you/your team/your business at the end of the coaching?
◆ What are the expectations the organisation has on the outcomes of the coaching?
◆ How will your line manager measure the success of the coaching?
◆ What are the different array of measures we might use here?
◆ From these, which are most appropriate for this assignment?
◆ Which ones are most valuable for you/your team/ project?
◆ Which ones will add most value and to whom?

- If your manager was here what would they be saying to you for what they need you to get from the coaching?
- What hard measures might we consider here?
- What needs to be the outcome/measure here?
- How can we make this (goal) measurable, so we know when you have achieved it? Stoltzfus (2008)
- What softer measures might we use to measure its success?
- What do we need to measure?
- What do you want to measure?
- What will be different when you have achieved this goal?
- If you were to look back in 6 months-time what might you have wished you had measured?
- Who do you need to speak to help identify the measures we need to consider?
- What leadership outcomes would be useful to consider here?
- What results do you want to see?
- What results do your team need to see/experience here?
- What does your manager/stakeholder need you to derive from this?
- How will you measure those outcomes?
- How do we translate these outcomes into tangible measures?
- If you were allocating yourself some measures/ outcomes here, what would they be?
- How do we measure this coaching?
- What team measures can we align the coaching outcomes too?

- What team measures/KPIs could we contribute to here?
- How do you differentiate the most critical measures from the rest?
- How do the team's KPIs influence our potential outcomes?
- If there was one measure we would like to include/ focus on here, what might it be?
- How will you know when/if you are being successful?

Changes—these look to highlight shifts in thinking and behaviours achieved during the coaching and how it is influencing performance back in the workplace. You can use them during the coaching assignment and at the end of it:

- What changes have happened in the workplace as a result of the coaching?
- What results are now different for you?
- What behavioural changes are now different?
- What are you experiencing now compared to before?
- What are you now doing that you weren't doing before?
- How do you view the situation compared to previously?
- What changes have others said they are experiencing with you?
- What is the evidence for you that change has taken place?

- What is happening for you in the workplace which shows you change has occurred?
- What kind of changes have occurred for you?
- What is the nature of the changes you have experienced?
- How embedded are the changes in your practice?
- What might be missing from the changes you have made so far?
- What is still missing from the changes you have made so far?
- What difference have these changes brought to your daily work/role?
- What shifts have you been noticing since the start of the coaching?
- Where have these shifts been occurring for you?
- What previously identified measures have now been met?
- How do you know?
- What is now different?
- What feedback have you had in relation to the measures and achieving them?
- What are the quantitative and qualitative changes you have experienced?
- Where are you now compared to where you were before?
- What different work outcomes are you now achieving?
- What is not different in your thinking and behaviours compared to the start of the coaching?

TOP 10 MEASURING SELF-COACHING QUESTIONS

1   What specific measures do I want to focus on?
2   How will I know I have achieved what I wanted to?
3   If I was coaching someone else, what measures would I expect them to come up with on this topic area?
4   What might be good hard and soft measures here?
5   What measures might my line manager expect to see here?
6   What does different look like for me personally at the end of this?
7   What change do I want to have achieved once I have coached myself?
8   What different behaviours/thoughts do I want to be demonstrating at the end of this?
9   How do I want to be moving forward?
10 What difference might others need to see from me?

UNDERSTANDING PROGRESS

UNDERSTANDING YOUR client's progress from the previous coaching session and throughout the assignment is critical. Newer coaches may often treat this progress review as quite transactional, an aperitif before the main coaching discussion. So, they just pass through this stage. However, there is significant learning value to be gleaned from your clients during this phase. This progress review phase may also influence the nature and direction of the subsequent coaching conversation.

Additionally, coaches may often not go beneath the surface of the progress that is shared with them. They simply accept it at face value. Exploring and understanding the reasons why the progress was or was not successful is important, rather than simply that progress has or has not been made. This exploration will reveal a lot about client motivations, priorities, commitment, thoughts, feelings as well as any themes to client behaviour.

Similarly, taking the opportunity to explore client progress from a 360-degree perspective, considering stakeholder insights might also be a powerful discussion or activity.

ALSO CONSIDER:

The use of **Person Centred**, **Stakeholder** and **Reflective** questions alongside Progress questions will assist in bringing out more learning from the client's experiences. The client may not naturally take on a reflective perspective so you might have to consciously introduce it to the conversation.

Progress to date—This is focused attention on what the client has been working on and how successful they have been in their achievements between the sessions. It also considers impact, reasons, themes and feedback within this progress:

- What have you been focusing on after our coaching session?
- Take me through what you have been doing since our last session?
- How have you been making progress in the past weeks?
- What are some of your wins and losses since our last meeting?
- What does this progress look like to you?
- What progress are you seeing?
- What progress are others seeing?
- What progress are you experiencing?
- What progress has been achieved versus what you were expecting?
- What kind of progress has/is being achieved for you?
- How have you been applying what was agreed in the session?

- What have you noticed the most about your progress?
- What has contributed to your progress?
- How has this contributed to your progress?
- How have they contributed?
- What have you been doing differently that has enabled you to make this progress?
- What have you been doing differently that has given you that success?
- What theme(s) are these to those things that have enabled your success?
- What have you not been doing that has impacted upon progress?
- How are you evidencing your progress?
- What have you not achieved so far?
- What specifically has not been progressed?
- Where is progress not being made?
- What progress is not being made?
- What progress have you made compared to where you thought you might be?
- What progress are you not happy with?
- What progress isn't being seen by others?
- What are the expectations around your progress?
- What has been the impact of your progress on your role/day to day work?
- How has your progress been making a difference to you/the team/others?
- Where has your progress had most impact?
- Who has your progress impacted?
- How much closer to your goal does this progress take you?
- How does it bring you closer to your goal(s)?

- How does this progress contribute to your goal(s)?
- What does your progress now bring you?
- What feedback have you been given on your progress?
- What feedback have you sought on your progress?
- How are you holding yourself accountable for your progress?
- How do you want me/your line manager to hold you accountable for your progress?
- How do we need to build accountability for progress into our conversations?
- How are you measuring progress back in the workplace on this?
- Where are you now compared to where you want to be?
- On a scale of 1-10 how much is the progress being made meeting with your expectations?
- On that scale what needs to happen to move you up it?

Mindset and emotional progress—alongside actual progress, exploration of shifts in thinking and emotions will give a key indicator of where your client really is. What has been happening for and to them behind their activities. Shifts or lack of shifts in these areas provide valuable insight and may require further exploration. It is important the coach explores this area as it will provide a deeper understanding of the client:

- How do you feel about your progress?
- How are you thinking/feeling about your progress?

- What do you think/feel about this feedback on your progress?
- How happy are you with your progress?
- What progress have you made in your mindset here?
- How is your mindset shifting as we move through the coaching?
- What physical/mental/emotional shifts are occurring?
- With us now at X session, how do you feel you are you progressing?
- If the roles here were reversed, what might you be thinking about the progress I had made?
- What are you now feeling as being different from the coaching you have received?
- What are you most pleased about with the progress you have made?
- What are you not happy about regarding your progress?
- What have you learnt from your progress to date?
- What do need to learn from your progress so far?

Obstacles to progress—where little or no progress is being made compared to what coach or client expected, this needs to be understood more. It may be a one off, or a common occurrence, there might be reasons or excuses, in the client's control or not. Is there something deeper happening for your client? Either way, this needs to be examined and potentially resolved. If lack of progress becomes a frequent conversation, then the coach may have to remind the client of the coaching contract and even recontract:

- What are the things that have hindered your progress?
- What kind of hinderances were they?
- What has stopped or slowed your progress on the actions?
- How much of these hinderances were real or perceived?
- Which of these hinderances have been in your gift to change/overcome?
- What do these hinderances have in common?
- What is there to notice about these hinderances?
- What do you notice about these hinderances?
- What themes are there to any obstacles?
- What themes do you notice about these obstacles?
- In reality how much of a hindrance was it really?
- Which of these obstacles were in your control to change/influence?
- What did you do/not do about these obstacles?

Moving forward—once progress has been established, clarity around what this progress means for the client's goal(s), and future focus should be achieved:

- How does this progress impact on what you are ultimately trying to achieve?
- How does this progress influence the nature of our future focus and conversations?
- Following this progress what are the next steps for you?
- Following this progress what needs to happen?
- Following this progress what do you want to have happen?

- If we take this progress away from your original goal, what is now left to focus on?
- How does this progress influence or change the focus of your goal?
- What further actions have now arisen as a result of this progress?
- What have you learnt about yourself from your progress so far?
- What thoughts or feelings have shifted for you as a result of this progress?
- How does this progress inform your thinking moving forward?
- What about this progress might we need to discuss further?
- What might be missing from the progress you have made to date?
- What mental/emotional shifts do you still need to make to keep momentum?
- How does this progress influence the rest of our coaching?
- How do you overcome these obstacles in the future?
- What needs to happen to avoid these obstacles happening in the future?
- What progress do you want to have achieved by next time?
- What does your future progress look like?
- What does your future progress here need to look like?
- Considering progress so far, where does your progress need to be next time?

TOP 10 PROGRESS SELF-COACHING QUESTIONS

1 What has changed in this area since I last spent some time exploring this area?
2 What am I doing that is feeling different?
3 What different results am I getting?
4 How am I progressing against my chosen measures?
5 What different behaviours and thinking am I demonstrating that others are commenting on?
6 What feedback have I asked for to learn from?
7 If I stepped out of myself and looked back what would I now be seeing?
8 How do I now think and feel about things that are different to how I was before?
9 What has shifted in my mindset about this?
10 What do I now need to do to move further forward with this?

SCALING FOR INFORMATION

SCALING IS a commonly used and simple coaching technique. It gets the client to rate something or a situation on a sliding scale, usually a number. Normally, scaling uses a range of 1-10. The focus of the scaling is where they are on the scale at present. Then, where do they want to be on the scale at the end of the session or coaching assignment. This then creates a gap to close or achieve and this is where the coaching conversation may well focus—the classic gap analysis.

Scaling allows you to remove emotion from a situation by making it a number, then identify the elements both of present and future situations.

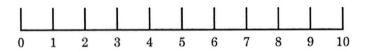

A lot of new coaches use scaling, but they only focus on identifying the numbers and never really explore further. 'Mining' deeper, beyond the numbers is where richness can be found, and a lot of uncovering is achieved. Examining thoughts, feelings, reasons, motivations, hopes and desires, creates powerful pictures for both parties. This exploration is helpful for both coach and client to develop a clearer understanding of the current and desired future state. Spending focussed time on scaling by the coach will also help identify qualitative measures that can be used with the client.

Where some clients are not comfortable with using numbers in the scaling other approaches can be used. A hot or cold scale, or even using colours can be tried. It is even more important when using these to fully understand how your client is interpreting the temperature or colour.

Present state scaling—aimed at determining the current situation of your client through their own eyes. Where they think or feel they are given all that has been happening around them. Also understand their reasoning behind that number. You look to build awareness from and with the client about experiences, thoughts, feelings, observations and feedback that leads them to the number they have stated. You may also provide evidence-based challenges to the client's choice of scaling number:

- At present out of 10 where are you at?
- At this very moment, where are you at the moment on a scale out of 10?
- What makes you say this number?
- What is happening for you to say this number?
- Describe to me what it is you are doing day to day as this number?
- You say you are X, it's not 1, so what is it you are doing well at the moment?

- The number aside, describe to me what this looks like in terms of behaviours, approach and language.
- Describe how an X leader behaves?
- As this number X, what do you recognise you are not doing?
- What is not happening for you as that number?
- What does it feel like saying you are X at this?
- What feedback have you had that might support this figure?
- What feedback have you had which might challenge this figure?
- What are you not currently demonstrating, which you need to move away from X?
- What behaviours are missing as an X?
- What impact does being X have on your work?
- How might the team scale you on this?
- How would your line manager scale you?
- What would your line manager be saying to me as evidence to support that number?

Future state scaling—here you are encouraging the client to envision where they might want or need to be by the end of the coaching session or assignment. Within this, gaining images of what their future state might look like from theirs or other perspectives is a form of visualisation. Helping them build a mental picture of their future state, brings it to life with descriptions of behaviours, actions and approaches. In doing so this helps create an emotional attachment to this future state, which will increase the likelihood of the client engaging and seeking to achieve it:

- Where would you like to be on the scale at the end of the session?
- What number would you like to be at by the end of the coaching?
- What does that X look like to you?
- Describe specifically what an X would look like for you here?
- What would an X feel like?
- As an X what would others be seeing you do?
- How would you come across as an X?
- What would you be doing differently as an X?
- What would your line manager expect you to be doing as an X?
- What are the team's expectations of an X team leader?
- What might you experience for yourself as an X?
- Who for you in the business might personify an X as a team leader?
- What kind of language would an X be using?
- How would an X team leader carry themselves in a meeting?
- How does an X team leader behave?
- How realistic is it for you to move from X to Y in the given timeframe?
- What are the stages to becoming an X?
- What's the first step to change do you think?
- What might be the logical steps to move toward an X?
- What knowledge or skills do you feel are currently missing, but need to have as an X?
- How achievable is an X?

- How much is an X a perfect scenario versus an ideal scenario?
- What would an X ideally look like to you?
- How much does your role need you to be an X?
- Where does your line manager need you to be on the scale?
- Practically, what number would your team need to see you at?

Gap analysis—once you have established where the client is and where on the scale they would like to be, a change conversation can be had. Work with them to develop their awareness and understanding of how they can move from their present to their desired future state. Identify what is required to move between the two states. Your questioning skill comes in being able to make any shift accessible and realistic:

- How do you move this forward?
- What might a stepped approach look like here?
- How might you break this X down into manageable steps?
- If you were to chunk this down to 'baby' steps what would they look like?
- What's the logical process here?
- How far away from a X are you?
- What needs to shift to become an X?
- What's missing in your leadership to achieve an X?
- What does the team need you to become an X team leader?
- How do you become an X?

- What new or different behaviours do you need to demonstrate as an X?
- You can't achieve an X straight away so what is the natural progression here?
- What is the first step looking like to you here?
- If you aimed for a 6 as a start toward the 9 what does this 6 look like?
- What differences, language, behaviours do you need to focus on for this 6?
- What's the starting point to move from here to there?
- Of the components of being an X which one(s) do you focus on first?
- Which of the future state skills will help you the most now?
- What are your gut thoughts about where you want to start?
- Who can help you to identify where to start?
- Based on previous experiences, what feels most comfortable to focus on initially?
- What steps need to happen before others?
- What can't be considered until later?
- Mapping this out in your head, where do you start?
- What are some of the interdependencies you have to consider when plugging the gap?

TOP 10 SCALING SELF-COACHING QUESTIONS

1   In relation to the situation where am I currently out of 10?
2   What is the evidence I have that tells me I am this number?
3   What is it like being this number, what am I doing/not doing?
4   Where do I want to be in a couple of months on the scale?
5   Where do others need me to be?
6   When I am there, what will be different about me and the situation?
7   How will I be thinking, feeling and behaving once there?
8   What are the natural steps to achieving this?
9   Breaking it down what are the components to bring the change I need?
10 What do I want/need to focus on first to move forward?

SYSTEMIC CONSIDERATION

YOUR CLIENTS don't work and live in isolation. They interact with and through other individuals and groups in their everyday environments. These 'others' influence and inform the client and can also be influenced and informed by the client. These influences include family, relationships and work 'systems'. Physicist and Systems Theorist Fritjof Capra (1996) recognised the importance of systems:

"The more we study the major problems of our time, the more we come to realise they cannot be understood in isolation. They are systemic problems, which means they are interconnected and interdependent."

If you are new to coaching the temptation is to just focus on the client in isolation, and not consider wider elements. Being purely client based in questioning only considers one person's views that impact one person. More systemic natured questions reflect the real world surrounding the client in which they are entwined with. It can be revelatory to both client and coach when their wider systemic world is opened up and examined.

John Whittington has pioneered systemic coaching and constellations, discussing it in detail in his book *'Systemic Coaching and Constellations: The Principles, Practice and Application for Individuals, Teams and Groups'*. Systemic questioning very simply focuses on exploring the systems and relationships the client might be involved and engaged in. Whittington (2016) states *'everything we are, everything we do, happens in relationship to multiple systems, multiple fields of information. So, we are systemic by nature. It is the same with our clients.'* Understanding the relationships, inter-dependencies, processes and dynamics between client and those around them is important. The hidden, the overt, the loyalties, the past, the present, the spoken and unspoken all influence your client's thinking and choices. Their work systems will include their team, department, line manager, the organisation and even external stakeholders. These systems will exist in their own right and overlap with other systems. By examining, exploring and understanding these systems new perspectives, insight and direction will emerge.

By recognising their system, their place in it, their involvement with it and the dynamic between them, clients can make more informed choices to achieve the results they need.

Systems, present and past, have a powerful influence over individuals and teams even though these systems are mostly unseen. Teams with long and established histories will have well established and historic systems which can be hard to understand, manage and change.

When you develop the awareness and confidence in asking more systemic natured questions, they open up a whole new area to add to your coaching practice. Bringing breadth, depth and potency.

Systemic questions according to Patzner (2019) bring several advantages, including:
◆ Recognition of dynamics in groups and teams
◆ Breaking fixed behaviour patterns
◆ Developing new creative solutions
◆ Producing fewer circular conversations

Client based systemic questions—the purpose here is to draw attention and abstract detail from the client's own system and immediately surrounding ones. This process awakens the client to exactly what is happening in their immediate environment and the other environments around them:

◆ How are your decisions received by the team/line manager?
◆ What is challenging about the conversations you have?
◆ Who do you have most discussions with?
◆ What is it about this person which makes these conversations easier?
◆ When you do/say things how does the team/line manager react?

- What is the nature of the conversations with your line manager?
- What is the relationship like with your line manager/team?
- Where does the power lie in the relationship with your manager?
- Describe your relationship with your line manager/team.
- What is it you do that drives the culture in the team?
- If you had a different relationship with your team/ line manager what would that bring?
- Who do you have around you to support you?
- What is important to you here?
- How do you want your team to feel when you share this with them?
- How might they feel?
- What do you feel about the team?
- What do you feel about your relationship with the team?
- What is it that only you can bring to the conversation?
- What do you bring to the team?
- What is it that only you can bring to the team?
- How do you influence this culture?
- What difference can you bring to your team?
- How does that influence/impact upon the team?
- How does your line manager/team influence your thinking and behaviours?
- How does what your line manager and team not do influence your thinking and actions?
- What difference can you bring to your team?

- How does that influence/impact upon the team?
- What is it that your line manager needs you to bring to the team?
- What is your role in this?
- What does your role need to be?
- What role does your team need you to fulfil?
- What role does your line manager expect you to play?
- What does the organisation need you to do?
- How does your role/position/thinking need to shift in relation to team/LM/stakeholders?
- What are the gaps in your role from a team perspective?
- How do you bring change here?
- What do you need to change in you before trying to change others?
- How will external change that you bring about impact upon you and this piece?
- Which of your skills are best suited to remedying the situation?
- What is your work and who does it serve? (Hawkins & Turner 2020)
- What really matters to you? (Hawkins and Turner 2020)
- If you don't make the change, what are the consequences short/long term?
- What small steps can you take to change the landscape?
- How will/might the team respond to your changes?
- What hinders your ability to influence?
- What would your key stakeholder(s) want you (and your team) to learn from this situation?

Team based systemic questions—The buil on the client-based questions, deeper examination of the team relationships, interactions, and dynamics with the client. The questions uncover thinking and awareness which might not be recognised, understood or acknowledged:

- Who has most influence on the team?
- Who has the most influence in the team?
- What influence do you have in the team?
- How do the team respond?
- What is not being said in the team?
- How does the situation affect the team?
- What might each team member say about this if they were in our conversation?
- How will the team be impacted in the future?
- Where does power lie in the team?
- What would each of the team value about your approach?
- What would members of the team want/need/ask of you here?
- Who is most impacted?
- How do you think you come across to the team?
- How might they view you/your leadership?
- What do the team members value about you?
- Who makes decisions in the team?
- What's the nature of your conversations with the team?
- What is the culture of your team?
- Who is the expert in the team?
- Who is the nurturer in the team?
- Who is the 'doer' in the team?
- What influences the team?

- How is it influenced?
- How does age influence the team?
- How does experience influence/impact the team?
- How does this experience influence the team/ culture?
- How does the make-up of the team influence its behaviours?
- Where does control lie in the team?
- What clarity might the team need?
- How does the history of the team influence you?
- What clarity does the team need to have?
- What clarity might the team be missing?
- What are the issues likely to be for the team here?
- Who is most concerned about the situation?
- What makes the situation better or worse?
- How are relationships impacted?
- How come the power lies there?
- What kind of power is this?
- How does this power show itself?
- How do you/the team respond/react to this?
- Who notices when you make decisions/actions?
- How does the culture present itself?
- What culture are you creating on purpose or by accident?
- What does the future need to look like for you?
- What shape does the future look like here?
- What does the future need to consider for you?
- How is the organisation influencing the culture of the team?
- What does the team think/feel about the organisation?

- How does the history of the team influence its dynamic?
- How does the history of the team influence its communication?
- Where are the loyalties in the team?
- Who are the team loyal to?
- How do you influence the loyalty of the team?
- How does the history of the team impact its performance?
- What legacies lie within the team?
- How do they manifest themselves?
- How do yours and the team's predecessors still influence you and the team?

Organisational systemic questions—These encourage your client to look up and scrutinise the interdependencies that lie between them and the organisational entity. Gaining clarity on what consideration they have given to organisational influence and interplay. They examine the implications, consequences and opportunities in the wider organisation:

- What is happening in the organisation that you need to consider?
- What might be the organisation's perspective on this?
- What does the organisation need of you here?
- What is the interplay between the organisation, the team and you?
- What is the relationship between you and the organisation?

- What is the history between you and the organisation?
- On a daily basis where does your focus lie—self, team or organisation?
- Where does it need to lie?
- Who else in the organisation do you have to be conscious of?
- Who else in the organisation can support you here?
- Who in the organisation do you need to influence?
- What is the organisation not telling you?
- What does the organisation need to know about this?
- When does the organisation not need to know?
- What does the organisation not know?
- If the organisation could speak to you, what might it say?
- What parts of the organisation might be most affected here?
- How does the organisational direction impact on what you want to achieve?
- How does the organisational direction influence your thinking/activities?
- How does the organisational direction need to influence your thinking/activities?
- What organisational activities/plans/processes will be influenced/impacted by your goal/ activities/decisions?
- Who in the organisation needs to be involved in the decision making?
- What are the organisations expectations here/of you?

- How is this decision/activity aligned to organisational thinking/strategy?
- How do you influence the organisation over this?
- What influence does the organisation have here?

External environment systemic questions—senior leaders especially need to have an eye both on what is happening outside the organisation and how the external environment and stakeholders informs business decisions. They also need to view the business through an environmental lens. They should develop accountability around the role that the client and organisation play in the external environment and society:

- What might be the perception of those outside of the business to this decision?
- How would customers perceive this?
- How does this business decision impact on people outside the business?
- What environmentally needs to be thought about?
- How have you considered the wider environment here?
- What is important outside of the business here?
- What is the organisation's environmental impact?
- How does the organisation influence outside of its walls?
- Where does the organisation need to influence externally more?
- How does the organisation influence externally more?
- What are the consequences for the organisation outside of its four walls?

- What outside the business do you need to be aware of?
- What social responsibilities do you or the organisation have here?
- How does the piece support or promote the organisation in a social or environmental way?
- What might be the wider consequences that you need to appreciate?
- Who makes up the organisation's external system?
- What might be the value of this system to you?
- What are your external accountabilities as an organisation?
- How are you doing in relation to those accountabilities?

Wider systemic questions—Involve taking a wider perspective and general examination of impacts, influences and considerations both on and from the client:

- What is this culture dependent upon?
- What is the history to the culture here?
- How does this history manifest itself now?
- Who else needs to be involved in these discussions?
- What can each of them bring to the conversation?
- What do they each need to bring to the conversation?
- Who can bring clarity here?
- Who is best placed to bring this clarity?
- Where does the ownership of this lie?
- Where should the ownership lie?

- What stops the ownership from being elsewhere?
- Outside of the organisation what do you and your team have to be conscious of?
- What issues are likely to be presented by the team/ stakeholders/others?
- How does it manifest?
- Who needs to be considered in this?
- What are the consequences of not considering these people?
- What is primarily affecting this?
- How is the situation being influenced?

Specific system questions—once a specific system is identified as having an impact, time can be spent exploring it in greater detail:

- What do you know about this system?
- What is it made up of?
- What are the relationships in the system?
- What are you comfortable and not comfortable about in this system?
- What causes you most pain in this system?
- Where do you feel you belong in this system?
- What do you know about this system?
- What do you not know?
- How does this system influence you?
- How does this system show itself in your work?
- What forces do other systems have on you?
- How do these show themselves?
- What resources does this system offer you?
- What opportunities are presented here?
- What is it like being in this system?

- What do you not like about it?
- What is currently happening in this system?
- What needs to happen to make a difference to you?
- What sustains and limits the relationships in this system?
- How does this system operate?
- What is your specific involvement in this system?
- Who did you replace in this system?
- What are you still dealing with from the former person in this system?
- How do people view you in this system?
- How much of the past still plays a part in this system?
- What parts of the past are still present?

TOP 10 SYSTEMIC SELF-COACHING QUESTIONS

1   Who else does this situation affect and how?
2   What is it about relationship(s) here I might need to be aware of and address?
3   How am I and others impacted/influenced by the situation?
4   How do I and we need to be, moving forward?
5   What/who is my success here dependent on?
6   What else do I need to consider outside of myself?
7   Who can I utilise here and how?
8   How will the environment around me change as a result of this?
9   What really matters to me here?
10 What are the wider implications here?

RELATIONSHIP EXAMINATION

RELATIONSHIPS ARE CRITICAL in organisations and to our clients. A significant amount of what clients need to achieve, can only be done so with and through the relationships they have or create. Relationships enable individuals, teams and organisations. They are the web of connections that each client is part of. Many issues in the workplace can be traced back to the relationship dynamic, rather than an individual issue. Relationships are closely related to systemics questions, in that it is often the interplay between the parties that needs to be explored and attended to.

The exploration of client relationships needs to be sensitively done. Many clients may never have really considered in any detail their working relationships, let alone discussed their role them. Asking your client to describe the relationship is one thing, exploring their role and commitment to the relationship is another. Some relationship questions may well require challenge and tackling from an array of angles, to get a complete picture and deeper understanding.

There can be a temptation for new coaches to 'skim' across relationships in their conversations. By pausing and taking time to explore the dynamics of the relationship will develop greater appreciation for the client. Often, clients are too close to the relationship to be able to see clearly or objectively. Persistence is key.

ALSO CONSIDER:

Blending Relationship questions with **Systemic, Stakeholder, Reflective, Feelings** and **Thoughts** questions will provide holistic and thorough scrutiny for the client. This enables them to have a more multi-dimensional understanding to help inform decisions and direction.

Relationship status quo—This involves exploring and understanding the relationship as it is now, looking at the situation, roles, perspectives, thoughts, feelings, roles and responsibilities in the relationship. You are looking to get a good grounding in how the relationship is presenting itself honestly with any bias examined and challenged. Establishing understanding at this stage develops comfort with the client, for when relationships are subsequently scrutinised:

- What is important to you about this relationship?
- How important is this relationship?
- What is important in this relationship?
- What does the relationship bring you?
- What does the relationship mean to you?
- What do you like about the relationship?
- What is your role in this relationship?
- What is the relationship dynamic between you?

- What is the dynamic of the relationship between you, the stakeholders/team?
- What needs to change in the relationship?
- How does the relationship need to shift do you think?
- What parts of the relationship need to shift?
- How has the relationship changed over time?
- Describe the history of the relationship.
- How did the relationship come about?
- What do you find frustrating in the relationship?
- What is it about the relationship that frustrates you?
- How has the relationship evolved?
- How is it evolving?
- What do you notice about the relationship?
- What are the differing sets of expectations around this relationship?
- How do others view this relationship?
- How do the different stakeholders experience the relationship?
- What are your thoughts and feelings about the relationship?
- How does X view this relationship?
- How do you think X views the relationship?
- Where does the power lie in the relationship?
- What is your status in the relationship?
- Where does equality lie in the relationship?
- How does the team view the relationship?
- How does your relationship here compare to others?
- What is different about this relationship compared to others?

- How much does the relationship impact upon the completion of the project?
- What is not happening in the relationship currently?
- What are the factors that affect the relationship?
- What internal/external factors influence the relationship?

Relationships and the client—examining the relationship in more detail from the client's perspective. You are bringing in more challenge around roles, thinking, mindsets and behaviours in the relationship. Pick up and scrutinise particular words used by the client to describe relationship. Looking at it from a 360-degree perspective, as viewed by others outside of it:

- What do you bring to the relationship?
- What do others bring?
- What might others say they bring which you might not see?
- How might you be impacting the relationship?
- What are your contributions to the relationship?
- What is it you are doing to help/hinder the relationship?
- How are you influencing the relationship?
- How do you need to influence the relationship?
- What value do you bring to the relationship?
- What do you notice you don't bring to it?
- What value do others bring that you need to recognise?
- How have your thoughts changed over time?

- How would the other person here view the relationship?
- What would the team tell me about the relationship they observe?
- If you were in their shoes, how might you experience the relationship?
- If you were holding a mirror to the relationship, what might you see?
- If you put the relationship under a microscope, what would be revealed?
- What are you not doing in the relationship?
- How much are the issues here to do with you?
- How much are you part of the problem or solution here?
- What behaviours are you demonstrating towards others in the relationship?
- What might others say about your commitment to the relationship?

The future relationship—Here you help your client apply a future focus lens on the shaping of the relationship(s) for the future. You encourage the client to understand needs, behaviours, conversations and actions required to create the relationship they want or need:

- What do you need from the relationship?
- What do you want from the relationship?
- What does the relationship need from you?
- What do you want this relationship to look like in 6 months?
- What does this relationship need to look like?
- What is going to be best for this relationship?

- What is best for this relationship?
- What are the options for this relationship?
- What direction does the relationship need to take?
- What direction do you want to take this relationship?
- How do you need to develop the relationship?
- How can you develop this relationship?
- Where does the relationship need to be?
- What do others want from the relationship?
- What conversations have been had about the relationship?
- What conversations need to be had around this conversation?
- What conversations are you going to have about the relationship?
- Who are you going to have these conversations with?
- How do you bring change to the relationship?
- How do you express your views/thoughts/feelings on the relationship?
- How will you approach the other person in the relationship?
- What do you need to consider when approaching them?
- When might be the best time to do this?
- How does this relationship need to be?
- Describe what the relationship could look like in the future.
- What would be different in the relationship when/ if it changed?
- What does your contribution to the relationship need to be moving forward?

- What are the consequences of not developing the relationship to you/your team/your line manager/ your organisation?
- How might others expect this relationship to be moving forward?
- In 6 months-time, what will be different about the relationship?
- In 6 months-time, where does the relationship need to be?
- What is the future of the relationship?
- What can the relationship not look like moving forward?
- How do you want the relationship to be?
- What will be different about the relationship?
- What does the relationship need to look like in the future?
- What does a future ideal relationship look like for you?
- What's ideal for the relationship over the next few months?

TOP 10 RELATIONSHIP SELF-COACHING QUESTIONS

1   How much is the relationship where I want it to be?
2   What is my role in this relationship, versus what I want it to be?
3   How do I want/need this relationship to be?
4   What might the other person think about our relationship?
5   What do I need to do to develop this relationship?
6   What behaviours do I now need to demonstrate more?
7   How do I start to develop the relationship?
8   What conversation(s) do I need to have with the other person?
9   How will I know if things have changed?
10 What are my first steps to this?

STAKEHOLDER AWARENESS

MANY OF YOUR CLIENTS will often view the world only from their own 'bubbles'. That's not disparaging them, it's something we all are guilty of. Clients think of things purely from their own perspectives. Viewing colleagues, teams, leaders and clients through their own lenses, experiences and values. They often have confirmation bias too, looking for opportunities to reinforce their held views of the organisation and wider world. Whilst there is value in viewing from this perspective, stepping outside of this bubble provides an enriching perspective and opportunity for clients.

It is not uncommon for a majority of 'normal' work conversations to not even consider stakeholders and their impact. Questions and answers identified are mostly inwardly focussed towards the team and individuals, rather than toward connections and people who their work actually serves. In coaching, increasingly there is an encouragement to lift the focus away from self (client) to stakeholders and the wider system and how your client adds value to these.

The coach has a responsibility get the client to view the situation, issues, opportunities and direction through different lenses. Examining them through the eyes of differing stakeholders. Opening up wider insights and empathy, bringing a clarity never realised before. Subsequently helping them make more informed, balanced and considered choices.

> *"The stakeholder approach to business sees integration rather than separation, and sees how things fit together."*
>
> JOHN MACKEY, FOUNDER OF WHOLEFOODS.

Whole coaching sessions can be had exploring all the different aspects of stakeholder identification, engagement, communication and management. The use of activities and exercises in coaching sessions provides fertile ground for stakeholder questioning, exploration and understanding.

Finally, part of exploring Stakeholders is also about examining the strength of the relationships. A weak relationship may lead the client to be taken advantage of. Medium relationship may lead to it simply being one of transactions between parties. Only a strong relationship will mean there is more equality, and increased influencing of the stakeholder.

ALSO CONSIDER:
There is a strong alignment here with **Systemic** questions. Various stakeholders are part of the leader or client's work systems. Understanding these clients can develop increased awareness of the elements and impact of the

system as well as how to impact it. Being able to identify and map out stakeholders then consider the different dynamics creates a 360-degree view of situations, people and relationships. *Standing by a forest you see a few trees. Get into a helicopter and fly upwards, you not only see the entire forest but you it its shape, contours, gaps and growth areas.* Solely inwardly thinking and focusing doesn't achieve this view.

Stakeholder awareness—by having knowledge of their stakeholders, their relationship, involvement and the dynamics, the client can begin to plan how to approach, work with and ultimately influence them as a group and individually:

- Who are your stakeholders here?
- How would you rate the importance of them to you/your work?
- How would you rate them from most to least important?
- How would you describe your relationship with each of your stakeholders?
- Which relationships have the longest history?
- What is the history to each of your stakeholder relationships?
- What is the dynamic between you and each of the stakeholders?
- How would you describe the dynamics between you and the stakeholders, individually and as a group?
- What is the relationship between the stakeholders?
- What might you need to be aware of between these stakeholders?

- What is strong or weak in your relationships with them?
- What are the reasons they are like this?
- Which relationships need the most investment?
- Who do you need to pay most attention to and the reasons for this?
- Who needs least attention and why?
- Where does the nurturing of relationships need to happen?
- How will you go about this nurturing?
- What needs to happen first here?
- What are the unique styles of each stakeholder?

Stakeholder conversations—This involves developing an understanding and challenging what stakeholder conversations have taken place, particularly their relevance, importance and experiences of these conversations. This is to gain clarity on the nature of these conversations and the implications of them for the client:

- What conversations have you had with stakeholders to date?
- What have been the outputs from these conversations?
- How have these conversations informed your thinking?
- How do these conversations need to inform your thinking?
- Which stakeholder conversations are the most important to have?
- What are the stakeholders not saying?

- What themes arose out of the stakeholder conversations?
- What do these themes tell you?
- How do these themes help you?
- During your conversations with stakeholders, what did you observe or experience?
- How were the stakeholders behaving during the conversation?
- What did the stakeholder not say to you?
- How are stakeholder conversations informing your thinking/planning/activities?
- What stakeholder conversations are still outstanding?
- What was the nature of the stakeholder conversations?
- What conversations have not been had?
- What have you determined from these conversations?
- What have you learnt about your stakeholders?
- What have they learnt about you?
- How has your view of the stakeholders now been influenced from these conversations?
- How did you approach the stakeholder conversations?
- How did the conversations make you feel?
- What have you learnt about yourself from these conversations?
- What have been your takeaways from these conversations?

Determining stakeholder needs—stakeholder conversations will inform the client of their stakeholder's needs.

These in turn inform client thinking and decision-making regarding approaches, language and management of stakeholders. Robust conversation here will reduce risk later by pre-empting situations:

- What is important for your stakeholders here?
- What do your stakeholders need to get out of this?
- How will you approach identifying your stakeholder's needs?
- What do you need to think about when approaching your stakeholders?
- What will they be expecting of you when dealing with them?
- How are you planning your approach toward them?
- How are your stakeholders feeling about this?
- What feedback can your stakeholders give you on this?
- Who are your important stakeholders?
- How do your stakeholder's needs differ here?
- If your stakeholder was in the room with you today, what would they be saying to you?
- Taking each stakeholder in turn, what does it feel like being them in this project?
- Taking each stakeholder in turn, how might each one be feeling about your decision?
- What are the priorities of your stakeholders?
- What are/might be your stakeholders top 3 issues/needs/requests/challenges here?
- What value does this bring to your stakeholder(s)?
- What value do you need to bring to your stakeholders?

- What additional value might your stakeholders be seeking?
- What is your accountability to your stakeholders?
- How do these priorities influence your thinking/ decisions/actions?
- Which stakeholders require more or less communication?
- What are the different approaches to communicating with the stakeholders?
- Which stakeholders require more or less communication/support/involvement?
- How are your stakeholders involved?
- How do your stakeholders need to be involved here?
- What conversations might the stakeholders be having amongst themselves?

Stakeholder influencing—next, there may be a strong requirement to influence stakeholders in order for the client to achieve the outcomes that they need or are mutually acceptable. The greater the understanding of the stakeholders, the easier it will be to develop influencing strategies. Stakeholders will need to be influenced in a multitude of ways and at multiple times:

- How will you map out the stakeholders involved here?
- How could you map out the stakeholders, their importance, needs, influence?
- What is your thinking behind how you have mapped out your stakeholders?
- How much influence does the stakeholder have over you or in this situation?

- How will you influence your stakeholders?
- How will you influence individual stakeholders?
- What might you need to consider when trying to influence the stakeholders?
- Who has knowledge of the stakeholders that might be useful to understand?
- How are the team being encouraged to influence the stakeholders through their individual work?
- What influence do you need to bring to your stakeholders?
- Who is best placed to help influence your stakeholders?
- Apart from you, who else needs to bring influence to these stakeholders?
- What do you need to consider when influencing your stakeholders?
- Whose role is it to influence the stakeholders?
- What role does the team play in this?
- What should the team be doing here?
- What are the areas you need to influence on/ around?
- Who do you need to influence the most/ differently?
- Where do you need to bring most influence?
- What are the areas you need to influence on/ around?
- What are the risks around influencing the stakeholders?
- What risks do you need to consider?
- What do you not know about the stakeholders which might impact on your success with them?
- What skills do you bring in the influencing process?

- What skills do you not have?
- What skills might be needed?
- What skills are best suited to these conversations?
- What information do you need to have to influence effectively?
- What information are you currently missing to be able to influence effectively?
- What do each of your stakeholders need/not need to know?

Challenge around stakeholders—it is important that your client has a firm grasp and confidence that they have considered all they can around their stakeholders and the dynamic between them. These questions set out to test the robustness of their stakeholder considerations:

- What does your stakeholder not want you to do?
- Which is more important here, your stakeholder's needs or your own?
- The consequences to your stakeholders are what, if you take this route?
- What is the impact if your stakeholders say no here?
- What are the consequences of not having stakeholder buy in?
- What are your reasons for not considering the stakeholders so far?
- Who are the other players in this? Stoltzfus (2008)
- How are you tailoring your approaches to the different stakeholders?
- How might this look from a stakeholders perspective?

- How much is your thinking aligned to that of the stakeholder(s)?
- How much is your stakeholder's thinking aligned to yours?
- How much does your thinking need to be aligned to your stakeholders?
- How much does your stakeholder's thinking need to be aligned to yours?
- Who has not been engaged with?
- What are the reasons for not engaging with them?
- What consideration have you given to the value the stakeholders are expecting?
- Who else needs to know here?
- Who else needs to be engaged/involved from a stakeholder perspective?
- Who has not been engaged with and reasons for this?
- What makes you the best person to work with the stakeholders?
- What awareness do the team have around the stakeholders/their input/engagement?
- What awareness do the team need to have of the stakeholders?
- On a scale of 1-10 how confident are you that you will get the outcome you want?
- What might improve these chances?
- What have you not considered here that needs to be thought about?
- If you were a stakeholder, what weak points might you see in your pitch/approach?
- How do you want your stakeholders to view you?

- What would you class as a success from these conversations?
- What is the minimum you need out of these conversations?
- What are you prepared to concede to stakeholders here?
- What if your stakeholders disagree/say no?

TOP 10 STAKEHOLDER SELF-COACHING QUESTIONS

1   Who are my stakeholders associated with this piece?
2   What is my unique approach for each stakeholder around communication, involvement, influence and requirements?
3   What might be my stakeholders needs/ expectations of me?
4   What do I need from my stakeholders?
5   How do I get the most from my stakeholders?
6   What do I need to be aware of regarding my stakeholders?
7   What is my approach to my stakeholders?
8   Who is best placed to support me through this and in what ways?
9   What do I need to consider before and during my stakeholder conversations?
10 What does a 'win' look like for me and my stakeholders?

BEING PERSON CENTRIC

THE PHRASE *'coach the person not the problem'* is well known in coaching. In essence it means you focusing your coaching around the client's mindset, feelings, behaviours, experiences and internal elements, rather than trying to fix the external problem directly. In trying to purely solutionise, find causes and solve the problem you risk creating a patch fix. One which might not resolve the situation permanently. When this happens often you end up dealing with the symptoms rather than the cause of the client's issue.

Instead, focusing on them as people looks at the heart of the matter, in more of a meaningful and deeper way. Many issues and situations require mindset and behavioural understanding and examination to bring sustainable change. Person centred questions bring focus and clarity to thoughts, feelings, beliefs and behaviours and what underpins these.

By enabling conversation around the whole 'person', it creates a very different type of conversation and language around it. In turn the client is likely to be more emotionally engaged and aligned, because they experience the coaching as being about them as people, not simply as an organisational resource.

By coaching the person your coaching conversation becomes very different in content, style and approach. So too your questions also need a different style and language to them. As soon as coaching questions include more 'you' based content the focus of the question and accountability shifts significantly. By simply changing the focus of the language of the question it changes the whole emphasis and meaning of it.

Whether a new coach or an established one, it is very easy to be drawn back and consumed in the moment with coaching the problem and try to 'solutionise'. Whilst your intent might be valid, it is not healthy for either party. It requires conscious effort to stay in a person-centred 'zone'.

COACHING TIP:
- Occasionally adding stronger vocal emphasis to the word 'you' in the question highlights where the ownership lies to the client.
- Slowing the pace of the question and being very deliberate in its delivery, will also bring more meaning and intensity to it.

ALSO CONSIDER:
Combining **Systemic** and **Stakeholder** questions with Person Centric ones will help bring tangible links between what lies outside of the person and the importance of what lies within.

Understanding self—the starting point requires you to invest time in helping the client glean a clearer picture of themselves, their motivations, purpose, thoughts and feelings. Then they will readily identify what it is that will bring more personal satisfaction. Meeting their inner needs, not just role or work ones. Many of these questions are deliberately personally challenging:

- What's important to you here?
- What's most important to you here?
- What personal challenges are you experiencing?
- What thoughts and feelings does the situation bring to the surface for you?
- What conflicts are happening internally for you at the moment?
- How are these conflicts manifesting for you?
- What is triggering these conflicts for you?
- How is this impacting on you?
- What strikes you most about this situation and what we have discussed so far?
- What are your strengths in this situation?
- What strengths do you bring?
- How do you capitalise on these?
- What is the importance of this to you?
- What are your personal requirements from this?
- How do you know you are right here?
- How right do you need to be?
- How has this specifically impacted upon you?
- What is challenging you the most?
- How is this challenge manifesting itself?
- What do you need to do to get more meaning from it for you?
- If you achieved this what would it mean to/for you?

- Where is this challenge impacting you the most?
- What does this mean for you?
- How do you need to be stepping up here?
- What do you lose that's important to you if you do change? Stoltzfus (2008)
- Where are your responses coming from?
- Your responses, are they head or heart responses?
- What led you to respond that way? Stoltzfus (2008)
- What might you be avoiding here?
- What might you being doing here that is stopping yourself from moving/wanting to move forward?
- What do you know about yourself already that might assist you here?
- What has been revealed to you through the feedback you have received?
- What is your body telling you here?
- Within this, how are you showing up in work or toward others?
- What congruence is there between your head, heart and body?
- What do you personally bring to the table/this situation/this issue?
- What do you not bring?
- What are you unable to bring to the situation/ solution?
- What energy do you bring to this?
- What excites you about this?
- When was the last time you felt excited about a similar situation?
- What did you learn from that?
- What satisfaction might you get from achieving this?

- How would this satisfaction impact you in work?
- What legacy do you want to leave your team with?
- What do you want your team to remember you most for?
- What do your team need most from you here?
- What experiences do you want to take from this project/work?
- How much are your personal values influencing your thoughts/feelings/actions here?
- How are your values manifesting in your response to this situation?
- What conflict might your values be bringing to the scenario/relationship?
- In your role who are you serving?
- What are the different ways you are serving your team/line manager/stakeholders?
- How are you serving those people you work with?
- How do you need to serve them?
- How does your work serve those outside the organisation?
- What conversations do you need to have that you are not having?
- What's stopping you from having those conversations?
- What are you here to do in your role?
- What about this is important to you?
- Who do you need to be?
- How can you create this?
- What does that mean to you?
- What does X mean to you?
- What do you care about here?
- What do you care about the most here?

Awareness and understanding—these questions are partially reflective in nature to bring more personal awareness and insight. With this comes a more responsive rather than reactive mindset toward decisions, behaviours and actions:

- What is happening for you here?
- What stands out to you here?
- What stops you from committing to this?
- What do you need to have happen to feel different about it?
- What are you trying to accomplish?
- Where are you getting stuck?
- What kind of 'stuckness' is this for you?
- What are some of the blockers you are experiencing?
- What is the nature of the blockers you are coming across?
- How does this need to change for you?
- What kind of blocker is it for you—mental, emotional, physical, physiological, personal?
- How much is this a mental or emotional stuckness for you?
- What value do you bring to this scenario?
- How can you use this value?
- Where best can you bring this value to the change?
- What influence do you need to bring here?
- What is the change you want/need to see?
- How much will this change bring to you?
- How will this situation impact upon you in the future?
- What do you need for the future?

- Describe what the solution will bring to you.
- What will you have at the end which you don't have now?
- Where do you need to look for the answers here?
- What needs to happen here for you to have the confidence in yourself/team/situation?
- What are your priorities here?
- How do your priorities differ from those around you?
- How do your priorities align with the team's/business' objectives?
- What is most important to you here/in this situation/for the team?
- What do you need to challenge?
- What do you need to challenge that you aren't currently?
- What will give you the outcome you want/need?
- What challenge do you need to apply, and to whom?
- What will this challenge bring you?
- What might this challenge unlock for you?
- Who do you need to challenge?
- Who do you need to challenge the most?
- What is not being currently challenged?
- What kind of challenge is going to work best with X?
- What do you need to consider before bringing this challenge?
- What do you already know?
- What assumption are you making here?
- What assumptions might you be making here?

- What is the idea which most appeals to you?
- What ideas appeal to you the least?
- What is it about that idea that appeals to you?
- How does that idea resonate with you?
- What does the future need to look like for you in this?
- What do you need to evaluate here?
- What could evaluation bring you?
- What will these changes now give you?
- What do you lose/gain by not changing?
- What makes this an effective approach for you?
- What makes this an effective strategy for you?
- What makes this an effective tactic for you?
- What insight do you currently have?
- What insight do you need to have?

Moving to doing—clients primarily engage in coaching to bring momentum and change toward achieving something or help remove 'stuckness'. Here, the questioning focus shifts to taking action. The questions are formed with focus on how your client wants or needs to be, and what needs to happen to achieve that. The ways forward are their ways forward, rather than generic or objective ways forward:

- How do you need to be in this situation?
- Describe how you want this situation to be, moving forward.
- What are the choices you need to make here for yourself?
- How do you influence this situation in the best way?

- How do you marry up the risk versus opportunities in this situation?
- What are you prepared to let go of here to achieve the outcomes you need?
- What kind of challenge do you need to bring?
- What might be your counter approach to this?
- What do you need to do here, that only you can do?
- What do you want to do here, that only you can do?
- What does the situation need of you to ensure progress happens?
- What does moving forward look like for you?
- What fears might they be around moving this forward?
- What do you need to do here to kick start this?
- What do you want moving forward to look like?
- What would your future self be driving you towards?
- What do you need to personally change here?
- What personal changes need to happen to achieve what you want?
- What is your role in this?
- What progress would be unacceptable to you?
- What would you see as good progress for you versus slow progress?
- What are the first steps you want to make here?
- Where do you need to start here for yourself?
- What would be an acceptable success for you?
- What progress would you like to see here that will change how you feel about the situation?
- What is your body telling you to do?

TOP 10 PERSON CENTRED SELF-COACHING QUESTIONS

1   What is most important about this situation to me?
2   What are all the thoughts and feelings associated with this situation for me?
3   What is most challenging to be here?
4   What will the 'new' situation bring me personally in the future that I may not have now?
5   What am I most noticing about myself and the situation?
6   What could I learn from this situation about myself?
7   What are the things uniquely in my gift/power here to change?
8   What can I bring to the table that will improve the situation?
9   How do I want to be in all of this?
10 What is going to be my greatest challenge(s) here/with this?

BRINGING CHALLENGE

AS A COACH you have a role in bringing challenge to the client, challenge to their thinking, mindsets, attitude, behaviours, approaches, patterns and norms. Challenge should be discussed in the contracting and at the same time gauging their receptiveness to it. Having developed a relationship and trust with the client you are uniquely placed to bring appropriate challenge. Deeper knowledge of the client will enable you to tailor your language and style when presenting challenge.

The use of challenging questions takes the client to places they might choose not to go to, be afraid of going to or not considered going. Perhaps not knowing how to go there even if they wished to!

Challenge should be done based upon the situation, learning, awareness and needs of the client. There has to be value or benefit to the client when the coach chooses to use challenge questions. Not challenge for challenge's sake or to satisfy your own curiosity.

Challenge should be done appropriately and judiciously. Going 'straight for the jugular' in the first session might provoke a reaction in the client and create a subsequent fear of opening up. Similarly, overuse of it might come across as being negative and produce diminishing returns. Looking for opportunities to challenge in low-risk areas in early sessions will provide the coach with real-time feedback on how it is received.

COACHING TIP
It is important here that the coach considers their tone, pitch, intonation and body language when challenging. The intent is to raise awareness and not 'finger point'. As such the voice, language and body should match, provide and present an element of safety for the client. In Transactional Analysis terms, challenge done in an adult way rather than parental one.

ALSO CONSIDER:
Challenge can be appropriate within **Progress** questions. **Framing** questions can also gain benefit from some challenge to ensure the right focus for the coaching conversation. **Relationship** questions can be supported by challenge questions to help uncover more deeply held thoughts and perceptions within the client.

General challenge—This involves bringing closer examination and awareness through probing and entry level holding to account. The purpose is to bring to the surface areas which your client has overlooked, not considered or procrastinated over. This may evoke slight discomfort or embarrassment within the client. If this happens it may also present further opportunities to examine the client's thoughts and feelings toward these situations:

- What is it you are not addressing here?
- How much are you stretching yourself?
- How much are you really giving here?
- On a scale of 1-10 with 10 being high, how much are you actually giving of yourself here?
- What is stopping you from giving more?
- What is it you are not sharing with me?
- What are you not telling me here?
- What's missing here?
- What is it you are not addressing here?
- How much of this is a perception rather than reality?
- How might your approach here be interpreted?
- What is not being brought to the conversation here?
- What conversations do you need to have with yourself?
- What conversation are you not having with yourself currently?
- What conversation are you avoiding having?
- Where is this procrastination coming from?
- What should I be calling out here?
- What do we need to talk about here that hasn't yet been approached?
- What do others expect of you here that might not be happening?
- What is yet to be uncovered?
- What inner conversations are you having which might be influencing your thinking and activity?
- What's the inner dialogue going on with you here?
- What do you need to stop doing and what do you need to start doing?

Deeper personal challenge—you are raising the bar here. This needs a stronger and trusting relationship to be in place to ensure it is received appropriately and meaningful responses are drawn out. You are bringing more assertiveness, highlighting the importance of the questions. The focus is to enable a more microscopic analysis with the client, perhaps bringing out more deeply held thoughts, assumptions and beliefs. The coach isn't letting the client get away with low level responses or flippant comments:

- If I was to ask you to challenge yourself here, what would you be challenging?
- In reality how challenging is this for you?
- How much are you really pushing yourself here?
- How much are you contributing to the situation here?
- How much are you part of the problem or part of the solution?
- We have spoken about what others are not doing here, what are you not doing?
- How are you not contributing to this?
- If others were looking at this situation, what might their feedback be to you?
- How much does this really lie with others?
- How much are you displacing onto others rather than taking control yourself?
- What are you displacing in this situation?
- How are you applying the same measures to yourself?
- What are you not admitting to here?
- What do you need to admit to yourself here?

- Where are these thoughts/feelings coming from?
- I notice that you haven't spoken about X at all, how come?
- You have mentioned X several times, where is this coming from?
- What are you not sharing?
- What are you holding back from the conversation?
- I sense that there is more to this than is being shared?
- What responsibility lies at your door in this?
- What might you be avoiding here?
- What might you subconsciously be afraid of?
- If there was something you might be afraid of, what could that be?
- What is it you need to step up more to in this situation?
- What is the elephant in the room in this conversation?
- Where do you need to be leading this?
- What is yours to now lead on?
- What does your leadership now need to look like on this?

TOP 10 CHALLENGE SELF-COACHING QUESTIONS.

1   What is it I am not allowing myself to consider?
2   Where am I afraid to go with my thinking?
3   How much am I taking charge of this conversation/situation?
4   What inner conversations am I having that are holding me back?
5   Where are these thoughts coming from?
6   What am I not contributing to here, that I need to?
7   What do I need to stop doing and start doing?
8   What would others expect of me here?
9   Where do I need to lead this?
10 What am I now going to do?

ENABLING REFLECTION

BECOMING A reflective practitioner is part and parcel of growing as a coach and leader. However, for many clients they might only incidentally reflect on situations or themselves. Rather than being more conscious and deliberate about it. Here, reflective questions deliberately bring your client's fuller attention to themselves, examining what they did, what that actually might mean for them and what it might mean for future thinking, behaviours, or action. Whilst questions naturally enable learning through raising self-awareness, reflective questions provide deliberate scrutiny of activities, reasons and meaning. They draw out deeper learning from their experiences.

The three sub-areas used here are an abridged version of Graham Gibb's (1988) Reflection Cycle. The questions can be used in isolation or as part of a complete reflection process. Some of your coaching sessions might need to be more deliberately reflection focused. Sometimes, side stepping into reflection creates opportunity to focus on something specific that is arising. Reflective questions take your client from an initial factual position to one of consideration and renewal. For complete learning to occur—to wring out as much from situations or experiences— the whole process should be used.

> *"Self-reflection is a humbling process. It's essential to find out why you think, say, and do certain things... then better yourself."*
>
> SONYA TECLAI, MUSICAL ARTIST.

Examining what happened—This involves bringing scrutiny to your client and examining in the moment something they did or said. The purpose here is to bring elements to the forefront of their thinking and develop a deeper consciousness about something to bring more awareness of the experience. In normal instances clients might generalise or mist out elements. The coach brings a magnifying glass to the situation for the client to see what unravels, and where the conversation goes:

- How do their thoughts/words resonate with you?
- Exactly what happened?
- Take me through what happened.

- What happened step by step?
- What did you do step by step?
- What do you notice about what happened?
- What do you notice about what you did?
- Whereabouts is this speaking to you the most?
- How did it happen?
- How is it speaking to you?
- What were you thinking and feeling at the time?
- What leads you to that thinking/feeling?
- What makes this important for you?
- Where might this affect you the most?
- What do you notice about what you have said so far?
- What do you notice about your behaviours?
- What do you notice about what others have been saying?
- What themes might be coming out here?
- What themes are there to your thinking?
- What did you notice at the time about yourself?
- What themes are you noticing about your responses?
- How does the situation sit with you?
- How was what you said received?
- How did the client respond?
- How did the client come across to you?
- What feedback was shared with you?

Evaluation of what happened—Work with your client to explore specifics of how the situation or experience impacted on them, and what it might mean to them or their situation. Look to see what the client can recognise and learn from their experiences. Now they are being more introspective, what resonates with them, what do they now see, which they weren't conscious of before? How do they think or feel about something? How does it affect them? You bring a 'mirror' to the conversation for the client:

- What does this mean for you?
- Where does this now leave you?
- What has now changed for you as a result?
- What difference has this meant for you?
- What does this mean for what happens next?
- Where are your thoughts now?
- How are you now feeling?
- What do you now notice about the situation/ experience?
- What can you learn from this situation?
- What are you learning about this?
- What meaning can you draw from your experiences?
- What learning can be taken from this?
- What do you need to learn from this in relation to your work/team/the organisation?
- Longer term, where does this leave you?
- How has this affected you?
- Where abouts in your body does this experience resonate with you?
- How does it resonate?
- What do you take from this?
- How is it affecting you?
- How will this affect you?
- How are your thoughts/feelings shifting?
- What lessons/observations can you take from this?

- What are you now noticing about yourself, having thought about this some more?
- What do you now notice that you hadn't before?
- What is being challenged by this information/ revelation?
- Who can best help you understand what happens now?
- What stands out to you the most about all of this?
- Who else is affected by this?
- What realisations might you now be having?
- What is now evoked in you from this?
- What is now resonating with you?
- What clarity do you now have that you didn't have before?

Taking action—having evaluated and understood more of themselves and the situation this needs to be translated into action. Work with your client to determine what now needs to happen, what direction they wish to take, or what this means for their future. How this informs the current situation and what future difference needs to be brought out:

- What does this mean for how you move forward?
- Based on this, what might your next steps be?
- How does this inform your picture of the situation?
- How does this help you move forward?
- What now needs to happen?
- What needs to change in your thinking here?
- How do you now balance the needs of the project versus you wants of it?

- With this in mind, what change will it bring?
- With this in mind, what change needs to happen now?
- How does this inform your future focus/actions/thinking?
- How does this inform what you do now moving forward?
- How does this inform how you move forward?
- What needs to come from this now?
- What needs to change/adapt in your thinking/behaviours/mindset/actions?
- Who else needs to know about this?
- How will this inform the relationship?
- What learning have you taken that now needs to be (re)applied?
- What steps do you now need to take?
- What steps now do you want to take?
- Which thoughts now need to translate into action?
- Now what?
- How does this reflection now influence your way forward?
- What have you learnt here that now needs to be actioned?

TOP 10 REFLECTIVE SELF-COACHING QUESTIONS

1 What have I been doing/not doing in this situation?
2 How am I being affected?
3 What am I learning about myself through this?
4 What stands out to me the most so far?
5 What has shifted in my thoughts, feelings and behaviours?
6 What will I start, stop and continue as a result of what I am learning?
7 What changes do I need to make as a result of my reflections?
8 How is the picture of my situation now being informed?
9 What do I now need to do as a result of this?
10 What do I notice about what I have been doing?

REFRAMING THEIR VIEW

REFRAMING IS a technique originating from Neuro Linguistic Programming and is often used in therapy situations. Often a client's view is influenced by the frame in which it is viewed. If that frame is given different perspective, the client's view may also shift. It involves getting a client to view a situation or person differently by changing its meaning often by recognising the positive aspects or outcomes.

Your clients may have a natural tendency to view situations through a more negative lens. Re-framing questions forces them to take a different, more optimistic perspective and turning negative thoughts into more positive ones. There is a commonly used quote from baseball player Andy Gilbert who is reputed to have said *'If you look for problems you will find problems. If you look for solutions you will find solutions'*. The power of reframing!

ALSO CONSIDER:
Reframing questions can work well in conjunction with **Stakeholder** and **Systemic** questions to assist with developing and influencing awareness in the client.

Reframing own views—Work with the client to open up their thinking and see alternative perspectives, especially more positive if they are presenting a negative view. Potentially bring challenge or feedback to the conversation:

- How else might this be viewed?
- How could you consider this differently?
- In what way could you see this as a positive?
- How do you view this as an opportunity?
- How do you need to consider this?
- How do you need to view this differently?
- How else does this need to be viewed?
- If you were to look at this from the opposite side, what do you see?
- What is the alternative perspective on this?
- What view do you need to take on this?
- What would you need to have to view this differently?
- What might good look like here?
- What is the positive side of this?
- If you received feedback saying you were taking a negative view, how might you view it more healthily?
- To achieve success here how do you reframe your thinking?
- How do you need to view this instead?
- If you were to consider the complete opposite, what would that be/look like?
- How might you positively interpret this?
- What shift in perspective needs to happen here?
- If you could come back in 6 months-time and share learning with your present self, what might you be saying?

- What if you flipped that perspective, how might it be viewed?
- If you were to flip this around how could you view it?
- Give me a 180 view of this, what is it?
- Put this on its head, how do you now view it?
- If you were to walk completely around this view/ issue what might you then see?

Reframing and the perspectives of others—use stakeholder's and other's views as a point of reference to bring further dimensions to your client's views. Enabling the client to step out from their normal, perhaps more entrenched thinking:

- What might your line manager's spin on this be?
- How might your manager want you to view this?
- How do others expect you to see this?
- How do the team need you to see this?
- What might be an expert's take on this?
- What might be the team's view of this?
- What could be your stakeholders' position be on this?
- How might an expert in this encourage you to consider it?
- What do your team need your position on this to be?
- How might your organisation hope you view this situation?
- What should the organisation's slant on this be?
- How do you need to consider this in light of the team's/organisation's needs?

- Putting yourself in the other person's shoes, how do they see it?
- How can you see this from the perspective of others?
- If you mapped out your stakeholder's view on this, what would they be seeing here?

REMOVING BLOCKERS TO PROGRESS

UNBLOCKING QUESTIONS aim to help your client break patterns of thinking, challenge normal mindsets to enable movement forward in thinking or action. It challenges how the client is thinking or approaching something. This is also about getting the client to tap into facets of creativity and thinking they have, but might not ordinarily consider. It helps them view things more observationally and critically, helping the client to 'see the wood for the trees'.

The coach may have to work hard to create questions appropriate to the situation and in a way that the client will understand and respond to.

Unblocking can be about breaking a situation down or positioning it in a different way to enable the client to see through, around or even over it, to change it. Sometimes it can be as simply as a nuance in the question or how the question is asked that either maintains or removes the blocker. Examine the situation from alternate, parallel or even reverse angles.

COACHING TIP:
Within unblocking questions, the use of silence is very important. Giving your client the time and space to

think and process is invaluable. Create opportunities following your challenge or question for the client to come to the table. Stepping in too soon might be counter-productive, shutting down lines of thought and opportunity.

ALSO CONSIDER:

Combining unblocking with occasional **Socratic** or **Creative** questions can further interrupt normal lines of client thinking approaches. Developing an understanding of what they do or don't know before then asking unblocking questions which might be more taxing.

Internal blockers—these entail recognising that internal thoughts, values, beliefs, experiences and habits can all hinder progress and change. Many clients often purely look externally for blockers. You instead, encourage the client to explore how they themselves might actually be hindering or sabotaging progress. Your focus is one of attempting to raise the client's own awareness of internal factors, to then be able to bring about change or difference:

- How much is what you shared a perception you hold, or is reality?
- What do you notice about what you have just said/ shared?
- If others were hearing what you had just said, what might they actually hear?
- What are you not sharing here?
- If you were on the outside looking in, what do you see and not see in this situation?

- Who has the most influence here to bring about change?
- What influence do you have in this situation?
- If you could spontaneously do something here to remedy it, what would you do?
- If you had to make a decision now what would it be and why?
- How big a risk is it in reality?
- What needs to happen to make the risk more acceptable?
- What do you need to have to make the decision?
- What would you like to have to make a decision here?
- What would you need to have to make the decision easier?
- What is the risk of not doing something?
- If you were in my shoes, what would you be telling you to do?
- If we strip this back to its basics, what do you think this issue is REALLY about?
- What is the one thing we haven't considered yet?
- What is the one thing that is holding up the whole process/decision making/moving this forward?
- What are you not recognising in this situation?
- What do others perhaps see here that you aren't seeing?
- How do you need to look at this differently?
- How do you get a different perspective on this?
- How can you look at this differently?
- What emotions are stirred when you approach this situation?

- What are you doing/not doing which needs to stop or change to help this situation?
- What do you think/feel is holding you back here?
- What do you believe is in your own ability to change in this area? Stoltzfus (2008)
- What changes could you make that would make the biggest difference to what you are trying to achieve?
- What beliefs/values/thoughts/feelings are you holding which might be influencing you here?
- What do you need to change in yourself that would influence the situation?
- What changes could you make personally that would influence the here and now?
- What feedback have you received/sought that might provide you with more clarity?
- How much does this situation need to be resolved in the way you are thinking?
- What beliefs/values/thoughts/feelings are you holding which might be holding you back?
- How much are your behaviours part of the problem or part of the solution?
- What belief(s) about you or the team might be hindering you here?
- What might you not be sharing which we need to examine to change this situation?
- What has stopped you in the past from achieving similar?
- What might you be afraid of which we need to explore?
- What fears about the situation/person/relationship might be holding you back?

- What might 'unblocked' look like to you?
- What one thing might be key to unblocking all of this?
- What do you want to see here that you aren't?
- What are you not doing to help yourself achieve this?
- How do you conquer this once and for all?

External blockers—Bring examination and recognition to help determine factors outside of your client which are hindering progress. Walk them around and through the situation, with questions to help inform their view of possible external influences. This develops broader awareness and understanding within the client:

- If the main problem didn't exist, how would the situation look?
- What is the one thing that isn't happening here at the moment?
- How might others view this situation?
- What are the component parts to this situation/ issue?
- If we broke down this situation in all of its elements, what would they be?
- What is not on the table that needs to be?
- What is not being considered here?
- What needs to happen here that isn't currently?
- If you were to rate these areas as being the most to least importance, what would that look like?
- How might others rate them?
- What are the reasons they might rate them differently?

- What don't we know here?
- What don't we know at the moment?
- What do we need to know here?
- What do you not know that if you did would change your thinking/approach to this?
- How have you overcome similar situations before?
- What might not work here, but might be worth considering at least?
- What if this obstacle was removed, what would you do then?
- What is frustrating your progress at present?
- What is getting in the way of you moving forward with this?
- Which areas could make the biggest difference to the situation?
- What is standing in the way of you changing here?
- Where could you look to find the answer you need?
- Who has the information to help you answer the problem you are trying to solve?
- What do you need to have that you don't, to help you get traction here?
- Who has the clarity that might help you here?
- What resources could you tap into to overcome this obstacle? Stolzfus (2008)
- If you cannot find a way forward, what's the next best option for you/the organisation?
- What can you not change which you might need to let go of?
- What is REALLY making this difficult to achieve for you?
- In all of this, what is missing for you?

- What might you be resisting?
- What could you at least try and then see what happens?
- If you had to try something here, what would it be?
- What thing(s) could you try to break the stalemate a little?

TOP 10 UNBLOCKING SELF-COACHING QUESTIONS

1 What are the core blockers to change in this situation?
2 Which of these blockers are to do with me personally?
3 How might others suggest I might be a blocker here?
4 What themes do I notice with previous situations of mine?
5 How am I helping or hindering the situation?
6 What is not in my direct control that is blocking me?
7 What are the top 3 blockers I am facing?
8 What do I need here that I haven't got that will get some traction?
9 What might my stakeholders say is blocking me?
10 What do I need to make happen here that isn't currently?

THINKING AND FEELING

NEW COACHES ESPECIALLY, often shy away from exploring areas with the client beyond superficial and non-personal areas. Their questioning remains transactional, practical and about 'things'. Yet your client's behaviours, language, decisions and actions are determined by their thoughts, feelings and experiences. It is critical that you are confident enough to approach and uncover these deep, powerful drivers of your client's performance. Often it is the coach's fears or ignorance that stops them from questioning around thoughts and feelings, rather than their client's willingness to answer them.

The contracting conversation is a great place to appreciate how comfortable your client is in discussing these things. Discussing what value these questions bring to the client's awareness and learning is important. Listening and picking up on the client's words will give insight to their levels of comfort, or even asking them outright how they feel about sharing thoughts and feelings.

Continually investing in the coaching relationship will create a more receptive environment for these types of questions to be asked. Once the relationship has been developed, these questions will give you further confidence to approach and enter this thinking and feeling arena with clients. Some clients are more feeling-based than thought-based, or vice versa. It is for you to understand your client's preferences and develop questions accordingly.

Within the questions provided in this chapter, the majority have been created as feeling based questions. In most cases the word feelings can be simply swapped with thoughts.

ALSO CONSIDER USING:
These thinking and feeling questions work well alongside **Socratic** and **Person-Centred** questions. They help the conversation to become more accessible, personal and meaningful.

Present—Examine current thoughts and feelings and bringing out meaning and inference from them:

- How do you feel about the situation?
- What is making you feel this way
- This feeling is caused by what?
- What do you feel when you face this type of situation?
- What are the triggers for these feelings?
- How long have you felt this way?
- When have you felt like this before?
- Who have you shared these feelings with?
- What are these feelings like?
- In what situations have you experienced these different thoughts/feelings?

- What normally happens when these feelings occur?
- On a scale of 1-10 what is the strength of these feelings?
- When have they been less than this?
- What makes these feelings an X do you think?
- When they are an X, what do you notice about them?
- What correlation do you notice about the situations and your feelings?
- What was different then?
- What kind of feelings are these feelings?
- Whereabouts in your body do these feelings originate?
- How would you describe these feelings?
- What feelings do you have about this?
- What are you thinking about at present that you are not sharing?
- Where do these feelings stem from?
- What are you afraid of?
- What do these feelings tell you?
- What can you learn from them?
- What do you need to tell me about how you are feeling?

Reflection on thoughts and feelings—Help clients re-examine thoughts and feelings, drawing out their own observations of these:

- What do you notice about these feelings?
- What themes have you noticed about these feelings?

- What reflection have you done on these feelings?
- When are these feelings at their strongest/weakest?
- When do you really notice them?
- What creature do you associate with these feelings?
- How does this creature behave/walk/talk/express?
- How have you utilised these feelings in the past?
- What have you learnt about yourself from these feelings?
- When do these feelings about the situation change or vary?
- What do you noticed about that situation compared to this one?
- When do these feelings NOT occur?
- When do these feelings appear the least?
- What situations have you had when these feelings have not arisen?
- What were you doing then?
- How did you deal with the situation then?
- What caused those feelings not to arise then do you think?
- What do you normally do when these feelings occur?
- How do you react to these feelings?
- What associations do you have with these feelings?

Impact—Develop client awareness and appreciation of how the thoughts and feelings impact upon themselves and others. This in turn draws out more awareness and learning:

- What is the impact of feeling like this about it?
- What are the consequences of these feelings for you/the team/the business?
- When do these feelings show up the most?
- Where do these feelings show up the most?
- How do you manage these feelings?
- How do these feelings impact upon your performance/relationships?
- What behaviours do you demonstrate when you feel like this?
- Where do these feelings show up the most in your work?
- Where do these feeling show up the most in your relationships?
- How would the impact of this make you feel?
- How do you think the impact of this would make you feel?
- What might be the longer-term implications of feeling this way?
- What might be the short/long term consequences/implications of feeling this way?
- How do these feelings impact those people around you?
- When do these feelings have least impact?
- What situations have you come across where these feelings were less apparent?

- How do you come across to others when you feel this way?
- What is the wider impact of these feelings?
- How might these feelings affect the team?
- How might these feelings influence how you view yourself/the team?
- How might these feelings manifest themselves in your words and behaviours?

Future—Bring a future focus to thoughts and feelings and how clients want to think and feel. Move them away from where they find themselves to create tangible transformation:

- How do you want/need to feel about it?
- In 6 months-time how do you want to be feeling about it?
- When you do bring about change here, how will it make you feel?
- What would need to be in place for you to feel differently about it?
- In this situation in the future how do you need to be?
- How do others/your team need you to be?
- What would be the best outcome that would feel best for you?
- Describe your ideal feelings for the future?
- What feelings do you have about this?
- What do you want to feel about the future?
- How would X future make you feel?
- Describe the future you want which you think would give you the feelings you need.

- What do you feel would be the best possible outcomes for you?
- How would this outcome make you feel?
- How will you manage these feelings in the future?
- How do you need to manage these moving forward?
- How will you reduce the likelihood of these feelings arising?
- How can you harness these feelings and use them?

TOP 10 FEELING AND THOUGHTS SELF-COACHING QUESTIONS

1   What am I most feeling and thinking about at present?
2   Where are these coming from?
3   What is changing in my thoughts and feelings during this?
4   What needs to change with these thoughts and feelings?
5   How do these manifest themselves in me and the situation?
6   What do I want to feel here and in the future?
7   How do I make this happen/make this shift?
8   What are the steps to these thoughts and feelings?
9   What outcomes do I need to help me think and feel differently?
10 How do my thoughts and feelings need to show up in the future?

GETTING CREATIVE

MANY PEOPLE and clients stick to well-trodden routes of creativity that work for them. Often relying on just a handful of approaches. Here, you are using your questioning approaches to stimulate creative thinking and variety for your client.

It is for the coach to demonstrate versatility in their questions to generate new, different or alternative ideas from within their client. Sometimes this requires an overt and distinct difference in questioning style. Sometimes it is simply a nuanced change of language and how the situations are viewed. It requires a challenge to the status quo and of the client's mindset, to get traction.

It is important that you have a flexible style in relation to generating client creativity. Repeatedly hammering at a situation is unlikely to produce results. As with clients, new coaches can have a tendency to slip into repeating the same half dozen questions trying to get a different approach or answer. This simply doesn't work and becomes repetitive for the client. It is like going to a country with a different language, and simply speaking louder and louder to get the person to understand you. New coaches often struggle to think of different or varied creative questions. So, it requires conscious effort by them to develop a repertoire of questions to generate creative thinking.

Some creative questions may seem a little unorthodox and even a little strange to ask for the coach. Regular practice here will reduce this discomfort and help manage these feelings.

Many new coaches often leave their previous work or life experiences 'at the door' and don't consider their use within their coaching. It is useful for coaches to bring these experiences in to help them in creative questioning. In previous fields of work how did they generate creativity? What have they tried before they could apply in their coaching? These can make their creative approaches more natural and relatable.

Adaptive creativity—rather than the client looking for total newness, encourage the client to see what they have already around them and amending or developing this in some way:

- How could you adapt what you have to give you a different outcome?
- What are you thinking about which might be hindering your thinking?
- What can you learn from what happened in the other situation?
- What shifts do you need to make to how you are to work towards this?
- What needs to happen to break the cycle?
- What are the similarities and differences to previous situations?
- What do you have in your repertoire or past that you could adapt to here?
- What's working already elsewhere that would be suitable here?
- What is transferable from there to here?
- What do you have around you that might be adaptable?
- What's been applied elsewhere that might be worth exploring for here?
- If you could pick something up from a previous situation or experience, what would it be?
- What could you adapt or use from a current process or piece of work and use here?

Logical creativity—These are a range of questions which 'prod and probe' your client on their immediate situation and opportunities. Turn over stones in the situation, developing a deeper scrutiny and awareness and seeing what is unearthed:

- What would really work for you here?
- What would a perfect solution look like for you here?
- What's your gut telling you might work here?
- What are you not considering here?
- What do you think is stopping you from finding ways forward?
- What is not on the table which needs to be?
- What is the easy way forward in this situation?
- Which is the more difficult route?
- What would the organisation expect you to do here?
- What should you not do here?
- What can't be used here?
- What do you need most right now?
- What would make this situation worse?
- What wouldn't you do here?
- Who has the answer to this question?
- What will be a game changer for you here?
- What is your ideal picture here?
- Describe your ideal to me.
- If you took a very radical approach here, what could you try/want to try?

Alternative creativity—Introduce an element of freedom to your client's thinking. Remove more barriers and encouraging them to be different and open in their approach and gain more licence to challenge existing norms that might be held:

- What is possible here?
- What are the possibilities open to you?
- What do you not wish me to ask you? (Coaching tools company)

- What can you change here, if not everything?
- If you were to compare this situation to another situation, what would it be?
- If you could reimagine this relationship how would you want it to be?
- Imagine if the problem was removed, how would that influence your thoughts/feelings?
- If you were writing a story about this situation, how might it end?
- What is the answer we haven't considered yet?

Free creativity—Remove all constraints to your client's thinking. Take them to a place through questioning where no boundaries are in place and linear thinking is not encouraged. Often take them to alternative places or contexts to 'play' with their thinking:

- If you could start afresh here how would you go about it?
- Starting with a clean sheet, what needs to happen?
- If you started with a clean sheet how would you go about it?
- If you started afresh, what would be different this time?
- Given unlimited resources, how would you approach this?
- In your ideal world what might the answer or options look like?
- How might someone at Google approach this task?
- If the same situation was being faced by a bank/ supermarket/engineering company, what steps might they take here?

- If you were going to try something here but weren't able, what would you be trying?
- I know you say you can't find a way forward, but if you did what would it be?
- If this situation was in a sporting context, how might it be approached?
- If you were to remove part of the problem and replace it with something, which would you remove, and replace it with what?
- What is something you wouldn't normally try or consider but might be worth a shot?
- What 'thing' are you thinking of at the moment, but might be afraid or uncertain of sharing?
- If you were a consultant in a business what would you be advising them to do here?

TOP 10 CREATIVITY SELF-COACHING QUESTIONS

1   What have I got already that I could adapt to fit this situation?
2   What is my ideal scenario here?
3   What might be a logical approach?
4   What would my stakeholders expect to see as a solution?
5   If I was to rewrite this from the beginning, how would I go about devising the solution?
6   Who do I know who has experience here, who could help me?
7   My perfect solution here would be...?
8   What should I not try here/would not work here?
9   What is a less than perfect solution but would give me a working solution?
10 What resources do I have to help formulate a solution?

UTILISING EXPERIENCE

EVERYBODY HAS experience which can be brought to bear to a situation, or they have people around them whose experiences can be used. Often this area is overlooked or not examined in detail by coaches or leaders. Exploring the client's background, former work, roles and previous situations is time well spent. Some clients feel they have no experience of dealing with the situation. Not only can the coach challenge this, but also 'dig' out nuggets of historic activities and encounters to see where there can be a transfer to current situations or challenges. By rephrasing your questions your client can be helped to identify what other experiences lie at their disposal through teams, colleagues, peers or even outside their organisation.

Internal experience—this examines the experience which they themselves can bring to the situation and developing confidence in this. It also draws out from your client what they can learn from the experiences they are having:

- ◆ Where does this experience leave you?
- ◆ How will this experience influence you?
- ◆ What experience do you not have?
- ◆ What specific experience do you bring to the table?

- What previous experiences can you share with me?
- Which of your experiences can you bring to the table here?
- What experiences might others point out to you that you have?
- If I looked at your CV, what experiences would I see that might be used here?
- What experiences do you bring from X or Y roles?
- How will you extract most value from this experience?
- What can you uniquely take from this experience?
- How does this experience compare to others?
- If this experience hadn't occurred, what wouldn't you have learnt?
- What do you need to take from this experience?
- What do you want to learn from this experience about yourself?
- What does this experience demonstrate to you?
- What does this experience mean for you?
- How do you draw learning from what happened?
- What knowledge and skills have you developed which might be useful here?
- What knowledge, experience or behaviours do you most need to bring to the situation/team here?
- What can you uniquely do here, that no one else in the business can?
- What previous experiences do you have had could be of value here?
- What experiences outside of your work might be able to contribute to this situation?
- What experience in life have you had that you could transfer?

- How do you tap into the experience you have?
- How do you transfer your experiences to this situation?

External experience—Encourage your client to develop a picture of what experience outside of themselves is available for them to utilise. Lift thinking up to create the realisation that there is significant experience at their disposal and try to identify the appropriate experience for their situation. It also considers reverse thinking around experience:

- What experience is needed here?
- Who has the most experience?
- What experience is missing?
- What experience have we not considered using here?
- What experience have we not considered as being needed?
- Who have we not considered here who has the experience to bring the change you want?
- What is the combined experience of the team?
- Who would you not normally call upon here, but who might be useful?
- What experience do the team bring either individually or as a team?
- What would be on your wish list of experiences needed here?
- Where does the experience lie?
- What experience is most needed for the situation?
- What value will this experience bring to the team/ situation?

- What is the risk of not having this experience?
- How will this experience reduce risk here?
- What do the team need to learn from this experience/what has happened?
- If you had the choice of experience from inside or outside the organisation, where would you go?

TOP 10 EXPERIENCE SELF-COACHING QUESTIONS

1 What experience does this situation require?
2 What experience can I bring?
3 What experience do I not have that I will need to find elsewhere?
4 What associated experiences do I have that might work here?
5 What experiences of mine might hinder what I am trying to achieve?
6 What gaps exist in my skills and experiences that I need to develop or bring in?
7 What skills surround me that I can utilise?
8 What is essential versus desirable when it comes to what is needed?
9 What can I get away with that doesn't need experience?
10 What isn't required here?

INSTEAD QUESTIONS

CLIENT THINKING can often be linear and predictable. As with reframing there is value in more directly challenging and forcing different thinking, outside of normal pathways. This in itself also helps stimulate more creative thinking. Whilst 'instead' questions are not designed to produce polar opposites to the status quo, they do attempt to bring real difference to thinking and outcomes.

When faced with an 'instead' question your client can feel awkward and may not know how to fully answer the question. The questions can force the client to often answer in the opposite which can be stretching for them initially. As coach you need to persist with their approach and provide challenge to the client where they aren't fully answering the question.

COACHING TIPS:
- Rather than using pure open question prefixes at the start of the question such as 'What', the wording 'Describe to me...' may be perceived as being a little softer in approach.
- When asking these questions, you should bring strong vocal emphasis to the word 'instead', whether the word be at the start or end of the sentence. This highlights the focus and importance on the alternative.

- It is also important you use silence with clients. Giving them the time and space to process what the question is asking:
    - What do you want instead of this? (Mark McGuinness)
    - What do you want to be doing instead? (Mark McGuinness)
    - What do you want to be thinking instead? (Mark McGuinness)
    - How do you want to be feeling instead? (Mark McGuinness)
    - What do you want to be saying instead? (Mark McGuinness)
    - Where do you want to be going instead? (Mark McGuinness)
    - What does your team need instead?
    - What do your team need doing instead?
    - How do you want to be instead?
    - How do you need to be instead?
    - Where do you want to be instead?
    - Who needs to be doing this instead?
    - How does this situation need to be instead?
    - What needs to be considered instead?
    - What does this need to look like instead?
    - Who needs to be leading this instead?
    - How do you need to be instead?
    - Where do you think you should be/can be focusing your attention/energies instead?
    - Instead of this approach, what else is open to you?
    - Instead of using this language/style, what else might work?

TOP 10 INSTEAD SELF-COACHING QUESTIONS

1   Instead of this, what do I really need?
2   What does the situation need of me instead?
3   How do I need to be instead, to move this forward?
4   Instead of this, what alternate approaches can I take?
5   What do my stakeholders need here instead?
6   Instead of thinking like this, how do I need to think here?
7   Who is best placed to drive this instead of just me?
8   What should I be focussing on instead?
9   What other options should I be considering instead?
10 Instead of taking the lead here what should my role be?

BEING 'MAGICAL'

'MAGICAL' QUESTIONS take the client to a very different place of freedom in relation to how they are allowed to think. Often in organisations, the boundaries of what is 'allowed', or what common practice is, can be quite narrow and traditional. Systemic and linear practices around problem solving, thinking and collaboration. This stifles individual creativity. The purpose of these types of questions is to take your client to a place where there are no 'rules' around what is right or wrong, or what, or how things should be done. Transporting them to a place of thinking freedom, allowing them to be courageous and imaginative. Some clients may really struggle to think outside their own normal parameters. People who have a 'glass is half empty mindset' especially can feel they need 'permission' to think differently.

The challenge for you is to give yourself licence to ask such questions. A new coach, or 'traditional' thinkers may feel it a little strange or beneath them to take such an unorthodox approach to their questioning. Again, frequent use of these questions will reduce awkwardness and develop coach confidence in creative questioning.

These questions should be used sparingly and intermittently. Blended well with 'normal' questioning. Overuse reduces their effectiveness. The power of them comes from the surprise of asking them, almost catching your client unawares. At the same time your client might find it refreshing and liberating to be given a completely free rein.

Often responses to these questions can be flippant, or off the cuff. Some responses might need working through or broken down before the client sees the relevance and reality of them. Once asked, your skill as the coach comes in exploring their responses and being able to get them to translate and apply the ideas to their work situation. This in itself might require interpretation, adaptation and flexibility from your client.

COACHING TIP:
- Bringing a change in volume, tone and exuberance when asking the question will bring greater emphasis to it.
- Encouraging or even animated body language supporting the question will always bring a smile to your client's face as they receive the question.

- Using a whiteboard or flip chart or even post-it notes to capture and map out responses adds further to the creative atmosphere and change to the nature of the conversation:
    - If you could cast a spell and remedy the situation, what would it then look like for you?
    - If you could cast a spell and remedy the situation, how would you then behave?
    - What would you do here if you had a magic wand?
    - If a genie could grant you three wishes about this situation what would you ask for?
    - What would your favourite hero do in this situation?
    - What would you do to make things right if you had unlimited superpowers?
    - What would you best friend suggest you could do?
    - What would your hero say about this situation?
    - What would your hero do about it?
    - Suppose that tonight, while you're sleeping, a miracle happens. When you get up in the morning tomorrow, how will you know things have suddenly got better? Bungay Stanier (2016)
    - If you could do anything in the world here what would it be?
    - If you could go to a utopian version of the situation, what would it be like/behaving/doing/experiencing?

- What would be your wish for the best possible outcome here?
- If you had a supernatural guide, what might they be saying to you?
- If you came back from the future what would you be saying to yourself?
- If someone could pass on some worldly advice about this, from beyond the grave, what might it be?
- If there was a parallel world to this, where your situation was resolved, describe what is happening in that world?
- If you were to reshape or redefine yourself, what would the 'new' you look like?

TOP 10 MAGICAL SELF-COACHING QUESTIONS

1   If I had a magic wand here, what would I change?

2   What 3 things would I wish for here to help me in this situation?

3   How would my leadership coach be challenging me here?

4   If I came back to this situation in a year's time what would I have changed?

5   What advice would I seek from someone who had come to me from the future?

6   Which any 5 people in the world would I bring in to help me on this piece, and why?

7   If the situation was magically resolved for me and delivering results, what would have changed to make this happen?

8   What would my future self be critiquing over this work?

9   If I could give myself any knowledge, skills or behaviours to make a success of this work what would I give to myself?

10   Which top 3 issues would I wish away and why?

GENERATING ACCOUNTABILITY

ACCOUNTABILITY IS an area that can be easily overlooked and often seen to be the same as commitment. Whilst the two can be linked, they are different. Clients often don't fully explore their accountabilities to themselves and others. It is important during coaching conversations that your client demonstrates their understanding of both what accountability is, and the breadth of their accountability at various levels in the situation. A conversation about accountability can create a huge amount of awareness and realisation, which in turn influences commitment:

- What is the nature of your accountability here?
- Who are you accountable to?
- Who are you most accountable to?
- What specifically are you accountable for?
- What is only your accountability?
- What is your accountability to the team?
- What is your accountability to yourself?
- What is your accountability to your line manager/ stakeholders?
- What are the expectations from others looking like to you around accountability?
- What are you on the hook for?
- What is it only you are on the hook for?

- What are the differing levels of accountability here?
- What are the differing levels of accountability only you face?
- What are the differing levels of accountability you need to consider?
- What does accountability look like for the team in this?
- What accountability can you delegate?
- What are you accountable for here that is different to your day-to-day role?
- What accountability do you need to demonstrate?
- How does your accountability need to manifest itself?
- How does your accountability show itself to others?
- How does your accountability need to show itself?
- How might your accountability vary?
- What clarity do you have around your accountability?
- What is the nature of your accountability?
- What type of accountability is that?
- How does that accountability sit with you?
- If not your accountability, whose?
- What does your accountability need to look like here?
- What does this accountability look like on a day-to-day basis?

TOP 10 ACCOUNTABILITY SELF-COACHING QUESTIONS

1 What is my accountability here and to whom?
2 How appropriate is the accountability here for me in relation to what I need to achieve?
3 What is the type of accountability I have, or need to demonstrate?
4 How do I think and feel about this accountability?
5 How do others view me and my accountability?
6 How does my accountability need to show itself to others?
7 How do I make myself more accountable for this?
8 Who can I check in with about my accountabilities?
9 How might my accountability evolve as this piece progresses?
10 How am I holding myself to account in this?

UNDERSTANDING COMMITMENT

ONE OF THE core premises of coaching is about your clients committing to pursuing their own courses of actions following your coaching. Coaching will only be successful for the client if they commit to the process and the actions they agree to. The coach has a key role in gaining client commitment to their chosen courses of action. This commitment takes the coaching from simply an exploration of a situation, to a decision to act, which is critical for the client's coaching outcomes.

> *"Commitment is the foundation of great accomplishments."*
>
> HEIDI REEDER, AUTHOR.

A discussion about a situation is one thing, commitment to do and to change is another. It is imperative for you to have an array of questions that bring focus to their commitment to action. Also, to understand what their understanding of commitment looks like to them.

Where non-commitment situations arise, you also have a role in understanding what might be causing this, then helping to resolve this.

COACHING TIPS

Discussing commitment during contracting, with focus on commitment to the coaching and application from the sessions, will make future commitment conversations/questions easier to raise:

- What needs to be achieved and by when?
- What are you going to commit to?
- What does that commitment look like?
- What will be the evidence of your commitment?
- How will you commit to this?
- How will you feel if you don't achieve this?
- What does that mean for your commitment to this?
- What might hinder your commitment to doing this?
- How have you committed to actions previously?
- How do we move you from 'might do this' to 'will do this'?
- What is the shift you need to make from 'ought to do this' to 'will do this'?
- What do we need to do or discuss that would help you make a commitment to moving it forward?
- What does commitment look like to you?
- What commitment do you feel/think is expected of you as part of the coaching?
- How do you need to manage your work to allow commitment to happen?
- When can you commit to this?

- When will you get it done?
- How does your commitment need to show itself to others?
- What is the minimum commitment that is required here?
- Whilst there is a minimum level of commitment required, what commitment should you be showing?
- What has your commitment been to pieces like this before?
- With what you want to achieve, what commitment from you is required do you think?
- How do you need to commit versus how you want to commit here?
- What is the difference between what you need to commit to versus what you want to commit to?
- What is stopping your commitment?
- What is hindering your commitment here?
- How do you want to commit to this?
- What are the ways you can commit to this?
- Out of 10 how committed are you to this course of action?
- What needs to happen for you to be fully committed to this?
- How do you feel about your commitment here?
- How committed are you?
- How committed do you need to be?
- How committed do you want to be?
- What commitment is expected of you by your line manager/team?

- What happens if you aren't committed to this?
- What is the impact of no commitment from you?
- What happens if your commitment changes?
- Who else needs to be committed to this?
- What does commitment from the team need to be?
- What commitment is required from your line manager?
- What stakeholder commitment is required?

TOP 10 COMMITMENT SELF-COACHING QUESTIONS

1 What is my commitment to this piece?
2 What commitment do others expect of me?
3 What does commitment look like for me here?
4 What is hindering my commitment to this/them here?
5 What will be my initial commitment here?
6 How do I build my commitment to this/them?
7 What do I feel/think about my level of commitment?
8 What do I want my commitment to look like?
9 What would total commitment look like here from me?
10 How much commitment is required from me to achieve this?

OTHER QUESTIONING ARENAS

WE HAVE MENTIONED questioning frameworks, types of questions and Socratic questions. There is also value in considering other questioning approaches for coaches. Their overviews are shared here for you and leaders to research and embrace as their needs and interest determines. Many of these and other approaches can work well in conjunction with the questions from the compendium. Familiarity with questioning frameworks will allow you to be able to experiment and develop your own questions.

APPRECIATIVE INQUIRY

Appreciative Inquiry (AI) is attributed to David Cooperrider and Suresh Srivastva in the 1980's. The principle behind it is very simple. In most situations where something is wrong or broken the approach taken is 'how do we fix this?'.

Appreciative Inquiry's approach is to take on a positive mantle and ask, 'what is already working here?' It focuses on the core strengths of an issue or situation. Taking existing strengths, achievements and successes, at an organisational or individual level and building on these. Whilst not ignoring past failures, it helps people work collaboratively to develop creativity and solutions. This positive approach is clearly brought out by Orem et al (2007) and their comparative sets of questions:

PROBLEM SOLVING QUESTIONS	APPRECIATIVE QUESTIONS
Tell me what the problem is.	What gives you energy?
Tell me what is wrong.	What do you most value about yourself?
What are you worried about?	What do you want more of?
What do you need help with?	What worked well for you before?
What's bothering you?	What's working well now?
What's working? What isn't working?	What first attracted you to...?
What are you going to do about...?	What did you do to contribute?

PROBLEM SOLVING QUESTIONS	APPRECIATIVE QUESTIONS
How are you going to fix this?	What does it look like when you... ?
What do you think caused this to happen?	How do you want to keep moving forward for yourself?

The 4-D Model was developed by Suresh Srivastva, Ron Fry, and David Cooperrider in 1990.

AI is often demonstrated as a 4-step process, all of which is formed around a positive core or affirmative statement.

Many clients can have a negative mindset around a situation. Coaches and leaders can begin to create questions focused on strengths, future opportunities and potential.

In doing so it encourages clients to re-interpret their personal thinking and narrative.

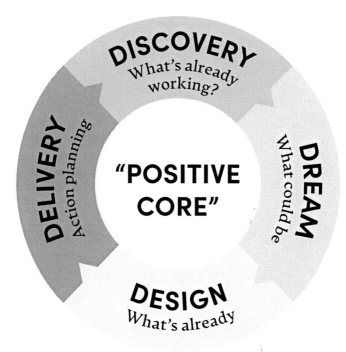

CLEAN LANGUAGE

Clean Language originated from the work of David J. Grove in the 1980s-90s during his work within the world of trauma. The purpose behind it was to allow people to express their own meaning around something without misinterpretation by others.

Every time we communicate, we use metaphors. These allow us to express ourselves in very personal ways.

Within each metaphor lies significant detail and personal meaning to us which can be explored. Great personal understanding and value can be understood by peeling the layers and depth expressed in metaphors. Clean Language is used when working closely with someone to understand THEIR meaning behind THEIR metaphors, without (mis)interpretation by others. Clean language helps to make more complex abstract ideas more accessible and tangible for both client and coach.

Grove developed a number of Clean Questions. These questions were free from the questioner's own metaphoric language, assumptions and interpretation. The 'cleaner' the questions the more valuable they are in unlocking the person's metaphorical world.

Whilst the Clean Questions are simple in nature, practice is required to consistently apply it. There is no deviation or amending to the 12 questions.

Rees McCann on his website shares these core Clean Questions:

DEVELOPING QUESTIONS

- What kind of X (is that X)?
- Is there anything else about X?
- Where is X? or (and) whereabouts is X?
- Is there a relationship between X and Y?
- When X, what happens to Y?
- That's X is like what?

SEQUENCE AND SOURCE

- Then what happens?
- What happens just before X?
- Where could X come from?

INTENTION QUESTIONS

- What would X like to have happen?
- What needs to happen for X?
- Can X (happen)?

Whilst the coach does not have to create their own questions, they do need to understand the core Clean Questions and when to use them. They can be used solely as pure set of clean questions, or as individual questions interspersed with other questions. When used as a pure set of Clean Questions they have the power to uncover great depth and meaning.

This approach also requires the coach to be aware of body language and varying pitch and pace of their language. This develops congruence with the how the client is coming across in the conversation.

For coaches, the use of Clean Questions allows them to park or let go of their 'baggage' (assumptions, leading, ideas, answers, biases etc) which might normally infiltrate their questions. This allows the client to fully bring their own meaning into the conversation. Enabling them to express themselves in ways they will never have experienced before.

Coaches are encouraged to undertake Clean training to develop familiarity with the questions and the power of metaphor.

PATTERN RECOGNITION AND EXPLORATION

All of our lives revolve around habits and patterns. From waking up in the morning, to how we carry out our meetings. We have repetitive patterns of interactions with others and our environments. Patterns are built from experiences during our lives—personal and professional. Something happens and we respond, this gets repeated and reinforced, happening at multiple times in multiple ways. These often unconscious patterns sustain us by enabling us or protecting us. For example, if your client approaches a senior manager in a certain way which is appreciated by the manager, the client is likely to repeat this with the manager again and again.

Patterns exist in relationships, toward 'things', emotions experienced with individuals and groups.

If a client is observed, even for a short time, their preferred and particular language, attitudes, mindsets and behaviour patterns can be recognised. This includes healthy ones which enable, as well as unhealthy ones which limit or disable.

Recognition of patterns provides fertile ground to explore with the client. When observed or stated in coaching sessions, it is likely that these will also be played out in relationships and the workplace. Similarly, patterns that are noted in an individual may also be reflected as patterns in wider teams or environments (and systems). They can be identified, explored, understood and where appropriate, changed. Bringing these patterns to the consciousness of the client helps remove the 'stuckness' they may experience in situations.

The coach's ability to observe these patterns, listen, then hone and tailor questions toward the individual to reveal patterns is critical. Finally, being conscious at questioning these patterns. Tunnelling, unearthing reasons, emotions and thoughts behind them. Helping the client to be more present and aware to manage potentially unhealthy patterns in the moment.

Providing feedback and challenge to the client on what they notice about themselves brings further consciousness around patterns. Ably developing the areas that Joseph Luft and Harry Ingram (1955) in their Johari Window model, refer to 'Blind spots' and the 'Unknown'.

Question creation is key to transforming patterns in the lives of clients.

LIMITING BELIEFS

Limiting beliefs are simply a set of wrong assumptions clients have or make about a situation or reality, a set of beliefs that can limit their capabilities. They are often picked up early in life from parents, friends, teachers and others. Similarly, experiences clients have in their lives can create or influence limiting beliefs.

Self-limiting beliefs may come in the form of an absolutely held belief in something which is expressed to others. Or in 'the small voice' in clients heads, which brings in self-doubt. Examples of limiting beliefs include—'I'll never become a senior leader', 'I'm not good at presentations' or 'I can't run a marathon'.

The more these are embraced and reinforced, the greater the impact on clients. If they keep saying to themselves that they can't do this or that, so that becomes their new norm, less able to separate fact from fiction. They appear to be real for clients.

The more clients become aware of their limiting beliefs, the better they can challenge the logic they are built on, therefore reducing their impact. They can even re-write their internal dialogue, creating new, healthier belief patterns.

Like pattern recognition, the coach is uniquely placed to observe and recognise limiting beliefs. The coach and their questioning techniques play multiple roles in these limiting belief situations:

- Challenge client thinking and language, testing their words, ascertaining if it is a truth or a limiting belief.
- Develop a recognition of the origins of the limiting belief.

- Discover the impact the beliefs have had on the client.
- Identify triggers for what might cause the limiting beliefs.
- How to recognise and develop strategies to prevent and manage them in the future.

The more ably the coach can deeply listen and tune into the client, the more they will recognise limiting beliefs. Their questioning skills play a key role in bringing these beliefs to the surface before then, helping the client recognise and manage them.

REFERENCES

www.thecoachingtoolscompany.com

Anderson LW, Krathwohl DR, Airasian PW, Cruikshank KA, et al. (2001) *A Taxonomy for Learning, Teaching, and Assessing: A Revision of Bloom's Taxonomy of Educational Objectives*. New York: Longman.

Bloom, B. S.; Engelhart, M. D.; Furst, E. J.; Hill, W. H.; Krathwohl, D. R. (1956). *Taxonomy of educational objectives: The classification of educational goals*. Handbook I: Cognitive domain. New York: David McKay Company.

Bungay Stanier, M. (2016) The Coaching Habit Say Less Ask More & Change the Way You Lead Forever. Canada. Box of Crayons Press.

Buckley, Dani (2018) *The Power of Asking Questions as a Leader*. The Center for Sales Strategy.

Cambridge online dictionary https://dictionary.cambridge.org/dictionary/english/question

Capra, F. (1996). The web of life: A New Scientific Understanding of Living Systems. New York. Anchor Books.

Downey, M. (20053) Effective Coaching: Lessons from the Coach's Coach. Texere. Penn State University.

Gibbs, G. (1988) Learning by Doing. A guide to teaching and learning methods. Further Education Unit. Oxford Polytechnic. Oxford

Goleman, D. (1995) Emotional Intelligence—why it can matter more than IQ. New York. Bantam Books.

Hannel GI and Hannel L (2005) *Highly effective questioning* 4th ed. Phoenix AZ: Hannel Educational Consulting.

Hawkins and Turner (2020) Systemic Coaching—Delivering Value Beyond the Individual. Routledge. Oxon.

Luft, J.; Ingham, H. (1955). "The Johari window, a graphic model of interpersonal awareness". *Proceedings of the Western Training Laboratory in Group Development*. Los Angeles

McCann, Rees www.reesmccann.com

McGuinness, M. www.thedesigntrust.co.uk

Morgan,N. & Saxton, J. (1991) Teaching Questioning and Learning. New York. Routledge.

Orem, S.L, Binkert,J. & Clancy, A.L. (2007) Appreciative Coaching: A positive process for change. San Francisco, CA: Jossey-Bass.

Patzner, H (2019) Systemic Questioning Techniques. Amazon

Stoltzfus, T. (2008) *Coaching Questions A Coaches Guide to Powerful Asking Skills*. Virginia Beech.

Srivastva,S, Cooperrider, D.L. Appreciative management and leadership: the power of positive thought and action in organisations. San Francisco. Jossey Bass.

Whittington, J. (2016). Systemic Coaching and Constellations: The Principles, Practice and Application for Individuals, Teams and Groups. Kogan Page